Running to Leadership
What Finishing
100+ Marathons
On All
Seven Continents
Teaches Us About Success

by
Anthony R. Reed

Running to Leadership

Disclaimer

Dedication

To our children and grandchildren. May they learn from my few successes and my many mistakes.

Acknowledgements

I extend my thanks and appreciation to Deborah Valrie for encouraging me to pursue my dreams and strengthening my faith.

For additional copies or bulk discounts, visit the web store at

www.Reed-CPA.com

Credit cards are accepted.

Running to Leadership

Copyright Notice

ISBN 978-0-9800215-6-1   (13-Digit)
ISBN 0-9800215-6-1   (10-Digit)

Running to Leadership: What Finishing 100+ Marathons On All 7 Continents Teaches Us About Success
Author: Anthony R. Reed, CPA, PMP

First Printing, February, 2011
Printed in the USA

Mr. Reed may be contacted for speaking engagements at

Anthony Reed, CPA, PMP
PO Box 180912
Dallas, TX 75218-0912
Anthony.Reed@Reed-CPA.com
www.RunningtoLeadership.com
Toll Free: 800-525-1668

MEMBER
NSA™
NATIONAL SPEAKERS ASSOCIATION

About the Author

Mr. Reed is an IT business professional and CPA with over 30 years of experience, including 25 years in management and executive positions. He's been featured in the business, IT, travel, and sports sections of major newspapers and publications across the country.

This includes the *Dallas Morning News, PMI Today, Runner's World, Southern Living, Ebony, Go,* and the *Journal of Accountancy.* He holds two graduate degrees (management and accounting) and two undergraduate degrees (management and mathematics).

He's also taught collegiate systems analysis, database design, accounting, and project management courses. He's also a certified Supply Chain Manager. He served on the Board of Directors for the Dallas White Rock Marathon, Oracle Applications Users Group (OAUG), the National Black Marathoners Association, software firms, and various local and international not-for-profit organizations.

His area of expertise has been analyzing and implementing financial, sales force, and manufacturing applications. He's led multi-million dollar, international projects for some of the largest Fortune 500 companies in the DFW area and worked for a Big 4 CPA firm in their management advisory division.

He has spoken at national and international project management, accounting, IT, and software quality assurance conferences. He has over 50 articles and four books published. The articles have appeared in *ComputerWorld, Datamation, Career Focus,* and *Runner's World* magazines. He's also been featured on radio, television, and podcast programs.

He's completed over one hundred 26.2-mile marathons around the world, including in over thirty States. He's won age group and weight division trophies along the way. In 2006, he joined an elite group of runners by finishing marathons on all seven continents. This included

2004 - Denmark's Tailwinds Marathon
2005 - Australia's Gold Coast Marathon
2006 - China's Great Wall Marathon
2007- Antarctica Marathon
2007 - Argentina's Fin Del Mundo Marathon
2007 - Kenya's SafriCom Lewa Marathon

Fewer than 225 people in the world had accomplished this feat. Subsequently, his journeys were chronicled in his book, <u>Running Shoes Are Cheaper Than Insulin: Marathon Adventures On All Seven Continents</u>. He resides in Dallas with his wife, Deborah, a triathlete, author, and minister.

Table of Contents

Running to Leadership

There's no "I" in TEAM.

**You're only as strong as
your weakest link.**

When in Doubt...Run!!!

A business analyst (BA) walked into my office and sat down. We spent several minutes discussing a problem, but we couldn't reach a resolution. Finally, she said, "You'll solve the problem during your lunch time run. Let's get together afterwards and you can tell me what you decided."

I was surprised by her remark. However, she was right: most of my problems *were* resolved after running. It didn't matter whether they were personal or business related. Running gave me the opportunity to see the "big picture" and to work through various scenarios and options. I also began seeing the long term impact of my decisions.

Running to Leadership

This may have something to do with running outdoors and not listening to portable music devices. When I run, I am completely unplugged. My mind is free to wander without any barriers or distractions. It was my opportunity to question the status quo and norms, analyze them, and challenge them head on.

For example, over the years, I had attended many team building sessions. The format was always the same.

First, we were sent to a "secret" offsite location, such a hotel or university. After our arrival, we were divided into teams. Next, we were given a task to perform within a certain time limit. This task rarely related to things at work. *[Reality Check: At work, you have a manager, who was hired based on their previous experiences and is there to provide direction. You rarely get to select your manager.]*

We've been asked to make devices that would prevent an egg from cracking when it's dropped, or we've played a game of Leapfrog with squares outlined on the floor with masking tape.

My last team-building activity involved building free-standing towers from balloons and masking tape. The tallest tower "won." *[Reality Check: Office politics and hidden agendas are rarely brought to the surface during these activities. After all, who would admit that they want to see the project fail for these reasons?]*

During the activities, the facilitator walks around the room and carefully observes the activities. *[Reality*

Check: Most of us are thinking about the unfinished tasks at the office. This is evident by the number of business phone calls and texting during the breaks.]

When the time was over, we were gathered back together and asked, "What did you learn from the activity?" At this time, we're frantically waving our hands like eager little children yelling, "Me! Me!" *[Reality Check: We've learned from previous team-building activities that the more we say, the sooner we may return to the real world.]*

Finally, someone says, "There's no 'I' in team." This is followed by a big group hug and high fives. We cross our arms, clasp hands with the person next to us, sway back and forth, and sing "Kumbaya." *[Reality Check: We know the real purpose of team building is to form a cohesive team by sharing timely information and building trust. Do you really need a full day of game playing to learn this?]*

I was frustrated after the last team-building activity. It seemed like a complete waste of time, so I decided to go for run. This fiasco stayed on my mind.

Why? The problems, which occurred prior to the team-building event, resurface in the individual(s) a few weeks later. The same individuals continue to make the same mistakes. This is compounded further by a lack of trust and understanding between the members. These *Individuals* are the "I's"" in TEAM.

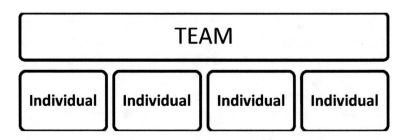

History tells us that the "I's" (*Individuals*) in TEAM cause project teams to fail. Furthermore, when the project team fails, the entire team is rarely fired. One or more *Individuals* are fired. This is verified easily by reading your newspaper's sports page at the end of a professional or collegiate athletic season. The losing coaches are usually fired before any players are traded or have their contracts terminated.

Strong teams are characterized best by the other catch phrase, "You're only as strong as your weakest link." In that light, it's more important to focus on the "I's" in TEAM for projects to be successful.

During my run, I mentally began writing TEAM. The first stroke was a vertical line for the letter "T." This vertical line was the hidden letter "I." This was the first I in TEAM.

As I continued writing, four "I's" were hidden in the word. There are four vertical, straight lines (or I's) used to build the letters T, E, and M. (You'll see later where each "I" represents an important component to building stronger individuals and, in turn, teams.)

Without the I's (or *Individuals*), there's no TEAM. Thus, to have a successful project TEAM, you must focus more on building strong individuals rather than building a team with one or more weak links.

As a leader, your role is to build strong individuals and facilitate trust between those individuals in order to implement successful projects.

TEAM

The glue that binds strong individuals into a TEAM is trust.

TEAM

TRUST - The glue that binds

Individual	Individual	Individual	Individual

A project team also consists of a wide variety of different talents, disciplines, and personalities. There may be technical people, functional staff, clerks, and warehouse workers. They're professionals who know how to perform their tasks — the subject matter experts (SME). In order for them to work together as a team, they must have trust.

The Cost of Trust

The glue that binds strong individuals together is trust. When trust is high, communication is faster and projects finish sooner.

When trust is low, communication is slower and projects take longer. This is a hidden (and very expensive) cost in many projects.

Consider two individuals who have to interact with one another. When there's a high level of trust, verbal commitments and, maybe, a handshake are all that's needed to "seal the deal." Verbal communication is not documented. If it is documented, it's not a large amount of paper. Emails aren't saved for eternity and meetings with "witnesses" aren't scheduled.

With a high trust level, individuals are able to expose their weaknesses and concerns to their counterparts without fear that they'll be used against them. Instead, their counterparts will work with them to turn weaknesses into strengths. Think of this as a highly supportive marriage.

Conversely, when two individuals lack trust, project cost and duration increases. Additionally, the volume of documentation (to support one's actions) dramatically increases.

Running to Leadership

Several entire industries and professions are based on mistrust.

- Attorneys are hired to draw up and review contracts.
- CPAs are paid to audit financial statements.
- Mortgage companies require a mountain of paper to close on a home.

I recall being in a project meeting where someone produced a four-year-old email to support his position. Imagine the amount of (and cost) of disk space used to store CYA emails.

I've witnessed people sitting next to one another using instant messaging to communicate. They wanted a "record" of what transpired. Perhaps you've seen a pair of cubicle mates sending emails to one another instead of just talking.

The "hidden" cost of these activities is increased storage cost, a slower network, and the hourly rate of the individuals, who are involved in these types of communication. Again, how long would your marriage last if you communicated in this manner?

Individuals have scheduled what should have been a two-person meeting with ten people to be their supportive witnesses. The lack of trust between the two main individuals cost at least ten work hours.

If there are 15 meeting during the project, you've wasted 150 project hours. This doesn't include the time to prep for the meeting or to decompress after-wards.

Think of a lack of trust on a project as two individuals who are involved in a messy divorce. They're advised not to talk directly to the other person. Needless to say, it becomes very expensive when you have to talk through your attorney and/or put all of your communication in writing.

Consider the case of a single developer on an IT project. She interacts with many individuals.

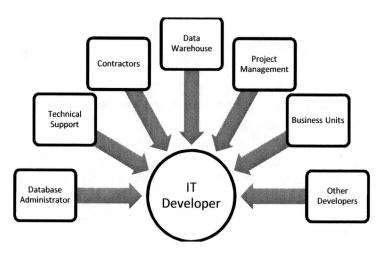

If she spends 5 percent of her time in mistrust management activities, she wastes "only" 2 hours per week. However, if this is extrapolated to the entire project team on a $5-million project, the estimated cost of mistrust is $250,000. On the other hand, on a 50-week project, this amounts to 2.5 weeks of project delays.

Running to Leadership

Building Trust

Building trust takes time. Here are a few pointers:

1. Keep your commitments, both big and small, and don't over commit. It's better to say, "No" or "I'll look into it and get back with you later" rather than making a positive commitment and breaking it at a later date.

2. Be on time. When you agree to attend a meeting, you're also making a commitment to be on time. One IT department lost its credibility and trust because its employees were always late for meetings. The other business units felt that if the IT staff was late for their meetings, then their business needs and requirements must not be important.

3. Don't try to be all things to all people. If you don't know the answer to a question, it's better to say that you don't know the answer but will find out. This is better than making up an answer and hoping that it's true.

4. Be respectful to all co-workers, from the people who clean the offices to the president. People who feel respected are more likely to trust you and work harder for you.

5. Learn to be a good listener. Don't open your laptop, "crackberry," or cell phone during a meeting. It

clearly shows that you're not giving the presenter your complete and undivided attention.

The Four I's in TEAM

People may have different reasons for being on the project team. However, they're individuals first and team members second. In order to get the most out of the team, you must also focus on building the individuals. What motivates an individual to be on the team? What motivates a person to achieve a goal?

The I's in TEAM represent important building blocks to create stronger individuals.

- Idea – You must define your goal.
- Incentive – You must be motivated to achieve it.
- Instructions – You must have a plan to reach your idea or goal.
- Implementation – You must be able to execute your plan.
-

They correspond to the elements of the Achievement Equation (aka GOMOPLEX).

I's in TEAM	Achievement Equation	Symbol
Idea	Goal Setting	GO
Incentive	Motivation	MO
Instructions	Planning	PL
Implementation	Execution	EX
		GOMOPLEX

Definition of a

TEAM

A group of individuals

who are	**I**ncented
to follow	**I**nstructions
in order to	**I**mplement
a common	**I**dea

- Idea – a plan of action; an intention.
- Incentive – Something, such as the fear of punishment or the expectation of reward, which induces action or motivates effort.
- Instructions – Detailed directions on procedure
- Implementation – to fulfill; perform; carry out; a means of achieving an end.

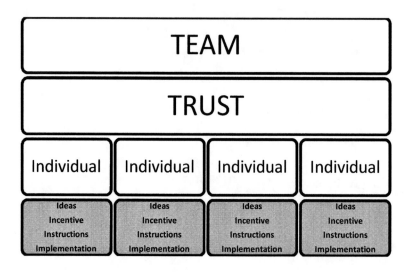

There are four components to the Achievement Equation. They were derived from communicating with successful project managers, refugee camp managers, professional athletes, marathon runners, endurance bicyclists, ministers, educators, mountain climbers, and executives.

The equation is multiplicative and the components are binary. That's to say that since each component's value is either zero or one, then failure to satisfy the requirements completely yields a value of zero. Furthermore, your answer, regardless of the other components' values, will be zero.

In mathematical terms, the Individual Achievement Equation is as follows:

14

Running to Leadership

$$I_A = I_G \times I_M \times I_P \times I_E$$

I_G – Idea (Goals)
I_M – Incentive (Motivation)
I_P – Instructions (Plans)
I_E – Implementation (Execution)

Where I_G, I_M, I_P, and I_E are binary.

The Team Achievement Equation becomes the following:

$$T_A = I_{A1} \times I_{A2} \times I_{A3} \times I_{A+} \times Trust$$

If any of the equation components are not completely implemented, you achieve nothing. Thus, you must completely implement each component to reach your goal effectively and efficiently.

These concepts were used to implement a $12-million project for $2.6 million, climb Mt. Everest, and complete exotic marathons in Antarctica, on the Great Wall in China, and in a Kenyan game reserve.

Non-work related personal accomplishments lead to stronger, confident, and more focused project team members. Recall when you were a youth and wanted to play outside, you had to complete your homework AND it had to be correct. Since you were passionate about playing, you focused on completing your homework assignment.

Your motivation wasn't to get a good grade but rather to play outside. We see the same effect when employees have a scheduled vacation. However, they can't depart until their work is completed and verified. They're highly motivated to complete their assignment so they can have fun.

This same principle applies to your project team members. A job is something that people have to do in order to survive. No matter how it's packaged, it's still just a job. Few of us have jobs that we're really passionate about. (If you won the lottery, would you continue going to your job?)

Thus, I found that encouraging and facilitating my team members to follow  their non-work-related passions led to more focused and engaging individuals at work. They wanted to complete their work assignments correctly (the first time) so they could pursue their real passions.

These passions included spending more time with their families, automobile racing, completing degrees, mountain biking, playing music, international travelling, and evangelical or missionary work. Furthermore, the lessons they learned from following their passions

were applied at work and essentially created a better environment.

For example, during a hot, high altitude, Kenyan marathon, cheetahs, and rhinos were roaming freely during the race. The same stress-management techniques, which were used during the race, were applied to managing highly visible, multi-million dollar projects at work.

My role as a manager and executive was to facilitate communications and trust between the I's (individuals) on the team. My other role was to resolve problems that stood in the way of their speedy progress.

Figuratively speaking, I gave the team high performance racecars and all of the responsibility associated with them. They could drive the cars as fast as their talents allowed. My role was to remove the speed bumps on the track.

The goal-setting component stresses personal scope identification and management. This, in turn, keeps you focused on the right personal and professional objectives during highly pressured engagements.

If you've ever worked on a project in which a team member died or suffered from "burn out," you'll understand the importance of establishing true individual priorities and objectives.

Running to Leadership

The top priority, whether running 26.2-mile marathons or climbing Mt. Everest, is to live. It's not to finish the race or to reach the summit.

About 80 percent of Mt. Everest deaths occur on the descent, not on the ascent. This understanding changes the emphasis from reaching the summit to surviving the entire round trip.

This same principle applies to managing projects. You must focus on all aspects of the project, including post-production support and maintenance. And you need to focus on what happens to your team members when the project has concluded.

The Achievement Equation's motivational component emphasizes the importance of understanding an individual's moral compass. What incites you to move while others are complacent? Or what makes you stay while others are fleeing?

For example, what motivates an underpaid employee who has highly marketable skills to come to work and complete a major project with full knowledge that their company may be closed? And they weren't offered a financial incentive by the company? At the same time, other employees were leaving for better, more secure positions.

You must have a moral reason to keep you motivated to achieve your goal. It's also important to note that not all people are motivated by the same stimulus.

Running to Leadership

 In the aforementioned example, money was not a motivating factor for the underpaid, dedicated employee.

Project managers must look beyond money to learn what motivates themselves and their team members. Motivators include time off from work, awards, better health, adventures/challenges, love, fear, and company recognition. This varies based an individual's personal needs and stage in their lives.

For example, the money spent to participate in the Antarctica Marathon did not motivate me to finish the race. If I was injured, such as suffering from frostbite, I was not going to risk losing fingers or toes in order to finish. Money was the very least of my worries. I could always earn more money for another trip, but I couldn't replace my limbs.

Money did not motivate me to keep moving during the race. It was the fear of freezing to death if I stopped moving. Freezing to death, and not the cost of the trip, was a moral reason to keep moving. What are the moral reasons that will keep you or your team members moving in the right direction despite challenges to leave the project or perform immoral acts, such as falsely reporting a project's status?

The Achievement Equation's planning component addresses embracing and managing risk while building self-confidence along the way. Many of us are taught to avoid risks. Unfortunately, we tend to avoid risk by ignoring and failing to recognize it. This actually leads to unrealistic project plans and increases project stress.

All project risks should be recognized and documented. They may be gathered at special risk-assessment meetings, obtained from lessons-learned files, and/or while meeting with individuals, such as team members and stakeholders.

After the risks are identified, mitigation plans should be documented. This should include identifying the triggers, actions to be taken, and the individuals responsible for addressing the risk. Once the risks are addressed, the project team's stress level should decrease.

For example, during one project, we included the "beer truck" scenario as a major risk. This is when a key team member gets "hit by a beer truck" at the most critical time of the project and is no longer available.

A similar situation occurred on a project. A key team member was deported two weeks prior to cutting over to a new system. Fortunately, we had planned for this risk and successfully implemented the system without additional stress.

Running to Leadership

During the Great Wall of China Marathon, we ran on stretches of the wall where the ledges were about 5 feet wide, with 50-foot drop offs, and no retaining wall. Unfortunately, runners could pass (and possibly bump) you along those ledges.

Kenya's Lewa Safaricom Marathon was held in the Lewa Wildlife Conservatory. Wild animals, including rhinos and cheetahs, roamed freely during the race. We encountered them on the road the day before the race.

I was acutely aware of these situations going into both races. I had to develop and be ready to implement my contingency plans for these life-threatening encounters. Developing the plans in advance greatly reduced my anxiety.

Twenty Miles Is Half of 26.2 Miles

The individual goals are identified. The individual is motivated. The plans and risk assessments are completed. The final component of the Achievement Equation is execution. If you have a good project plan, execution appears to be easy. However, it's important to pace yourself and your team members during the project and acknowledge the real halfway point.

Although a marathon is 26.2 miles long, many veteran runners consider the 20-mile point to be the half way-point, not 13.1 miles. During the first 20 miles, your work effort consists of 80 percent physical and 20 percent mental.

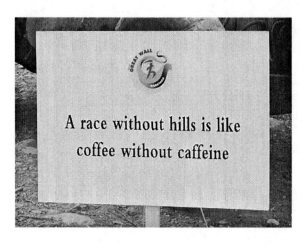

During the last 6.2 miles, your work effort becomes 80 percent mental and 20 percent physical. At this point, your body wants to quit, but your mind is screaming at your body to keep moving.

Due to the second phase, runners look for special treats to keep them moving past the pain and to focus on completing the goal. This includes everything from sponges and water showers to candy and cola.

Like a marathoner, the project team and individuals should not worry about events that they can't control. An experienced marathoner doesn't complain about the weather or the marathon course layout.

If they don't like the weather forecast or the number of hills on a course, they don't run it. They'll find a fair-weather marathon or a flat course. However, if they choose to participate, they don't complain. The only factor that you can control is yourself.

On a project, you can't control all of the factors. However, you can control your performance and mental outlook. You control your mental outlook by surrounding yourself with like-minded, highly creative, and motivated individuals.

Break fast menu:
hills and small rocks

Those people have positive outlooks and a "can-do" mentality. In this type of group, a problem situation is considered a challenge or an opportunity to excel. On a steep hill during an endurance race, we passed a small sign that read, "Hills build character." And so do challenging problems.

This also applies to addressing problems that occur during the execution phase. If you approach it with the right attitude, you'll make it to the top. One of the secrets behind endurance sports is having the ability to relax and think clearly while your body is under a great amount of stress. Another secret is pacing yourself for the long run. The knowledge that's gained from these lessons transfers very well to the work environment.

TEAM

Combining the components yields the Achievement Equation.

$A = I_G \times I_M \times I_P \times I_E$ (where G, M, P, and E are binary)

I_G – Idea (Goals)
I_M – Incentive (Motivation)
I_P – Instructions (Plans)
I_E – Implementation (Execution)

Where I_G, I_M, I_P, and I_E are binary.

By combining the four elements, a person can achieve personal and professional goals. And failure to consider any one of the elements means achieving nothing.

A simple way to remember the equation components is to think of them as parts of a multi-vitamin supplement. A supplement fills the gap between where you are today and where you want to be in the future.

The First I - Ideas (Goal Setting)

> *"Every new idea is an impossibility until it is born."*
>
> **Ronald H. Brown**

Bitten by the genealogy bug a decade or so ago I began to collect information on near and distant family members. However, a few years into my research, my system of manila folders—each neatly labeled with a separate branch of the family—had failed to keep pace with the volume and complexity of newly discovered relationships. (My great-grandfather had about twenty-five children.)

Running to Leadership

As a consequence I invested in a computer software package to map my family tree. Beyond the merits of its relational database the genealogy software yielded unexpected dividends in the form of self-reflection.

Like most people, I offered myself as the ceremonial guinea pig for the first entry and completed the usual fill-in-the-blank fields on the first screen.

- Name
- Place and Date of Birth
- Parents
- Schools Attended
- Last Known Residency

However, the second screen instructed users to write a short story about the family member. For the first time, I found myself asking:
- What do I want people to say about me after I'm dead?
- Which of my accomplishments or achievements will "stand the test of time"?
- Do I want them to say that I was good employee of XYZ Company for 30 years?
- Do I want them say that I was the best CPA or project manager?
- What will inspire future generations to overcome obstacles to achieve goals?
- What will live on after I die?

Running to Leadership

> "It's pretty hard for the Lord to guide you if you haven't made up your mind which way you want to go."
>
> – Mme. C.J. Walker

My answers to these and other questions ultimately led me to set and achieve ambitious goals. Ideas/goal setting is the first of the four variables of The Achievement Equation. As difficult as this component appears to be, it's the easiest one to complete. You simply state or write your goal.

Like many high school students, my goal was to go to college. And like many students, I completed that goal: I went to college, AND unfortunately, I got kicked out.

Surprisingly, this is the goal (i.e. "going to college") of many college dropouts whether they left in academic disgrace, in response to a family or personal crisis, or because economic hardship.

As my knowledge and contacts expanded, I refined my goal to *graduate* from college in *five years* AND to *earn* a graduate degree without failing or dropping a course.

Some people in the business world refer to the revised goal as a SMART goal.

Running to Leadership

Simple & Specific

Measurable

Achievable

Realistic

Timely

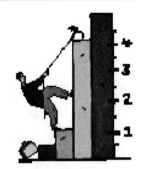

The simple goal of "going to college" failed the SMART test. The goal should have been to *graduate* from college within *five years*. This statement is simple and specific. The revised goal includes a five-year duration. Thus, it's timely.

Based on this timeframe, a student can determine the number of credit hours needed to pass each semester. The operative word here is "*pass*"—contrary to the conventional practice and language of "taking" classes. Thus, for a 120-hour degree program, a student needs to pass 12 credit hours per semester.

This measurement was very realistic. If the student studied hard, turned in assignments on time, asked for assistance when needed, and stopped wasting time, this would be achievable. The combined changes make for a SMART goal.

Organizers of large marathons often erect signs of encouragement along the course. During the Great Wall of China Marathon, we were about to run on one of the more treacherous parts of the course. A sign read, "Arrive in peace, not pieces." This simple sign became the overriding goal for many of my future achievements: to live to set other goals.

Arrive in peace, not pieces.

Annually, a small number of climbers die while trying to conquer Mt. Everest. Some of them may have felt the moment was their only opportunity. Regardless of the weather, their medical condition, advice from experts, or their climbing experience, they'll put their lives (and, at times, their fellow climbers' lives) at risk to reach their goal.

In "Why Are So Many People Dying on Mt. Everest?" (*British Medical Journal*, August 26, 2006), Dr. Sutherland wrote that once people see the summit, they believe they reach it AND return. Unfortunately, they run out of oxygen.

A few days before the Antarctica Marathon, the runners attended a banquet in Buenos Aires, Argentina. Fate delivered me a seat next to Jeanne Stawiecki. She was attempting to become the first woman in the world to have climbed the highest peak and to run a marathon on all seven continents.

Running to Leadership

Mt. Everest was her final jewel. She had two previous failed attempts. Her primary goal was not to reach the summit. It was to live. Her second goal was to reach the summit AND return safely. Undeterred, Stawiecki accomplished her goal on May 22, 2007.

Our dinner conversation helped me to prioritize my milestone goals for the Antarctica Marathon trip. Milestones are discrete incremental steps on your way to reaching a goal. It's possible to achieve most of your milestones and still miss your main goal.

Several years ago, I trained for a triathlon. It involved swimming, bicycling, and running. Race organizers set the swimming leg at a little over a half-mile in open water. This equated to a one-mile swim in a pool. Thoughts of the swimming portion resurrected a childhood dream to swim a mile.
I spent the summers of my formative years at camps. I progressed through the various swimming certifications. My dream was to be a certified lifeguard. However, I never developed sufficient endurance to swim the mandatory one mile.

The triathlon provided me the opportunity (or excuse) to satisfy my unfulfilled childhood dream of swimming one-mile. By race day, I had achieved the milestone. Unfortunately, events conspired to prevent my finishing the triathlon.

Running to Leadership

The Antarctica Marathon

Most runners adopted the following milestones for the Antarctica Marathon

- Stay alive. If they failed to finish the race, they could return and try another day.
- Set foot on the Antarctica Marathon starting line. So few people have touched Antarctica, that just being there was noteworthy.

- Finish the half marathon. Very few people have ever run any race on Antarctica.
- Finish the half marathon before the time limit expired. Once runners met this milestone without any problems, the ultimate goal was within striking distance.
- Finish the marathon.

In the evening, our group departed from Ushuaia, Argentina, on a converted Russian research ship named the R.V. Akademik Ioffe. We headed across the Drake Passage to King George Island, Antarctica. It was one thing to read about the Drake Passage's rough seas in a geography book; it was a completely different thing to experience it firsthand.

Running to Leadership

The 380-foot ship carries about 160 people, including the staff and crew. By comparison, the Disney cruise line ships are over 900 feet long and carry about two thousand people!

The accommodations, staff, and crew were great. The ship's crew informed us that we would either experience "the Drake Lake" (i.e. smooth waters) or "the Drake Quake" (i.e. rough seas). At breakfast the first morning, most of the passengers and the crew were sporting their motion sickness patches. I felt comfort in the notion of being one of many suffering that morning.

For this reason, I considered it an achievement just to be well enough to get to the starting line without suffering from seasickness, having any negative side effects from the motion sickness patch, and being able to keep down my food to have energy for the marathon.

Four times during the race, we had to navigate our way through 600 feet of ankle deep mud. Around the 3rd and 17th miles, runners encountered Collins Glacier, a sheet of ice at a 17-degree angle. (Most treadmills only go up to 12 degrees.) We had to run up three-quarters of a mile and run back down. If you slipped on the glacier, there was nothing to grab onto—except another runner.

Since I live and train in Dallas' mild winters and flat terrain, running up and down glaciers in sub-freezing temperatures, blinding snow, and strong winds was going to be a challenge.

Unlike the big city marathons, there were no buildings to shield you from the winds. You were completely at the mercy of Mother Nature. There was absolutely no place to hide.

Also absent from the bleak icescape were the cheering crowds along the race route. Your cheerleaders were your fellow runners, plus the penguins, fur seals, and skua birds. Occasionally, someone from the Russian, Chinese, or Uruguayan research stations would step outside to wave.

After the initial shock and awe of seeing Collins Glacier, it posed a physical challenge for both the ascent and descent. There were no real reference points, such as the end of a street block or building, to visualize progress, just non-stop snow and ice.

The 17-mile approach to the Collins Glacier challenges one's mental resolve. The endless landscape of ice and snow combine with physical exhaustion in ways that break down a runner's mental state.

Running to Leadership

This often results in a runner withdrawing prematurely from the race somewhat disoriented and dangerously exposed to the frigid cold as their body temperature drops from lack of vigorous movement.

Consequently, I adopted "keep moving" as my mantra. Stopping would have been hazardous to my health. Thus, the milestone of "keep moving" was directly related to my primary goal of staying alive. I completed the half marathon a full 20 minutes before the cut off time and successfully finished the marathon.

Eight days later, I also completed the Fin Del Mundo Marathon in Ushuaia, Argentina. Unforgettable!

Business projects fail primarily due to unrealistic scope (i.e. goals, milestones), timelines, and resources. Your team risks spiraling into an abyss where living another day is secondary to completing the project.

The project deadline minefield is littered with dead hearts (heart attacks), dead marriages (divorces), dead bodies (death), and dead working relationships (disgruntled staff members). If a project's scope is SMART and properly managed, your deadline will become party time.

Your Balanced Scorecard

One of the problems associated with achieving goals is that we can become too focused in one area and our life becomes disarray. We begin neglecting other aspects of our life. This can lead to a breakdown of our family structure, social circles, health, and faith. Thus, it's important to set goals in five areas.

1. Mental Goal – Stay mentally stimulated and alert. Challenge yourself to become a student every few years. Earn an additional degree or certification. Consider becoming a part-time, adjunct professor. Teaching forces you to learn new material well enough to teach it and answer questions. You may decide to read a book a month or complete your newspaper's daily crossword puzzle.

2. Physical Goal – A man was once so happy and relieved that he'd reached his goal, that he had a heart attack. The stronger you are physically, the more you can achieve.

Running to Leadership

A person might have a goal of running 100 miles a month. While this may seem like a lot to non-runner, this translates to about 30 minutes a day. Let's face it, most people waste more than 30 minutes a day. Also, the more physically fit you are, the more you will enjoy your retirement.

3. Social Goal – Schedule time with your family and friends. One of our goals was to have a family game night on Fridays. Some adopt a personal goal of never missing an event in which their children participated. Plan a weekly "date" night with your spouse. If you don't have your family's support, it may be difficult and/or costly (divorce) to achieve your goal.

4. Financial Goal – Money funds many goals and eases stress. The more money you have, the more goals you can achieve. Thus, it's important to set financial goals. Since you can't get a loan for your retirement, you should be saving for this event, while maintaining a high credit score. Financial problems kill most goals. While money may not buy happiness, you can always use it to wipe away the tears.

5. Spiritual Goal – This is the foundation of many people's lives and the biggest stress reliever. You may decide to attend your church, synagogue, temple, or mosque

weekly. You may decide to read a daily devotional or prayer. Others may decide to simply spend 30 minutes of "me time" or "quiet time" to re-connect with your inner self.

Crossing the Road

Distance runners spend a lot of time running on streets and roads. If you consistently run on one side of the road, you'll get injured. This problem occurs because most roads are curved to direct the rain runoff towards the sides of the roads and into the sewers or drains.

When a runner always runs on the left side of the road, their right foot is always higher than their left. Imagine running hundreds or even thousands of miles on a constant, uneven surface. You get the same effect (and problem) by running laps on a track in the same direction; your inside leg takes more pressure as you lean into the turns, and over time this leads to injuries.

The solution to this problem is easy: cross the road. You must spend an equal amount of time on both sides. In the case of track runners, run clockwise for a period and then switch to run counterclockwise.

This lesson was applied in my personal life and professional life and, subsequently, with my staff members. My academic and professional backgrounds were very technical: One of my undergraduate degrees was in mathematics, and I worked as a computer programmer (before later being promoted to a project leader and manager). I even taught collegiate courses in systems analysis, logical and physical database design, and computer programming. I was as one-sided as a person could get.

Technical   **Business**

During this time period, the news media reported that technical people had some of the highest divorce rates. What's more, business people weren't satisfied with the technical solutions that were being delivered. Executives were shocked at how quickly we were spending money, and we were experiencing a very high turnover rate in my profession. It wasn't unusual to have five jobs in five years.

I majored in math because I had terrible people skills. The computer was very predictable and forgiving; I could make the same mistake over and over again, and the computer would just spit out the same error message without ever getting mad.

I also realized that I couldn't take criticism in subjective areas. For example, I didn't like any course that involved writing a paper. The teachers didn't seem to understand what I was trying to convey. It was as clear as water to me, but as clear as mud to them. Years later, I realized that my grammar was horrible.

Running to Leadership

This subjectivity drove me crazy. A computer program, in contrast, was structured, used a limited vocabulary, and provided an almost immediate response regarding whether or not it worked. This was much better than writing subjective position papers or dealing with complex human emotions. My personal computer was as personal as I wanted to get in a relationship.

My lack of people skills forced me to cross the road to become a better husband, father, and project manager. I became more sensitive towards people's needs. I returned to college and earned a MBA in management. My newfound people skills became a very valuable asset. Our staff turnover rate decreased, and my employees were happier and more productive. However, my projects were still failing.

While attending meetings, executives repeatedly said, "You IT people just don't understand accounting!" I began to realize two important points: first, it's hard to build a system when you don't understand what how it functions; second, it's hard to manage a multi-million dollar budget when you can barely balance your checkbook.

This drove me to cross the road again. I earned a masters degree in accounting and passed the certified public accounting (CPA) exam. Crossing the road wasn't easy, but I was forced to admit that I had a problem. I could continue to run on the technical side and risk getting injured, or I could cross the road, overcome my fears, expand my horizons, and learn something new.

Running to Leadership

Over the years, I challenged my staff members to cross the road. They improved their soft skills, such as writing, presenting, communicating, and sales. They learned about the business units, such as accounting, supply-chain management, procurement, and marketing. Our projects became more successful.

Their approach to problem solving changed. Technology was not the solution to every problem. They began applying low-cost, non-technical solutions based on their business knowledge.

As CPA, I also ran a management consulting practice. It became evident that one of the major reasons for small business failures is the business owner's inability to cross the road. The owner may be a great engineer, craftsman, baker, or event planner, but unless they learn *all* aspects of running a business (for example, accounting, competitor and customer analysis, and PC skills) they'll fail.

The Second I - Incentive (Motivation)

> *"In every crisis, there is a message. Crises are nature's way of forcing change – breaking down old structures, shaking loose negative habits so that something new and better can take place."*
>
> **Susan L. Taylor**

How Motivation Entered the Equation

 Some of us are "pre-programmed" to set goals. A failing high school student will tell you that their goal is to graduate from college. Yet, they're not motivated to study for their high school classes.

An adult will tell you that they want a professional certification, such as a CPA. Yet, they won't make the time to study. Articulating the SMART goal was easy.

However, they weren't motivated to overcome the obstacles.

Self-motivation was essential for surviving and finishing the Antarctica Marathon. Unlike the televised marathons, such as the New York City Marathon, where you have over 35,000 runners with millions of screaming and supportive spectators, we had about 25 spectators and 200 runners.

Also, we faced obstacles unlike anything we had ever experienced, such as running up glaciers or being chased by fur seals. We also faced obstacles just getting to the race's starting line; crossing the Drake Passage. Thus, if you had low self-motivation or were unprepared for the obstacles, you would quit the race.

You had to be your own cheerleader and inspirational coach. Your mind had to tell your body to keep moving while your body was screaming at you to stop. Self-motivation propels you over the obstacles. It's important to surround yourself with self-motivated people. Self-motivation is infectious.

Weapons & Motivational Songs

My karate teacher disliked teaching weapons for self-defense. He felt that the weapons could become your crutch. If you found yourself in a street fight, the chances were great that your weapons were at home. Thus, he emphasized using equipment that you carry with you at all times: your body.

This same logic should apply to self-motivation. You should not depend on other people, such as family, friends, motivational speakers, posters, or props, like portable music players, to motivate you. The best motivator is your memories. They're always with you.

I've seen runners have emotional breakdowns during marathons because their MP3 died. The battery ran out of juice. The player got wet. It got damaged during a fall. The player contained their catalog of 150 motivational songs. Now, for the first time in their months of training, their motivator was gone.

It's better to memorize the motivational songs than to rely on a portable player. If you forget the words to the song, you can have fun making up your own version!!!

Self-Motivation Foundation

I believe that motivation is based more on fear rather than love. Even when motivation is driven by love, it may actually be the fear of losing the loved one that causes us to take action. Fear of poverty and homelessness drives me go to work, not the love of my job. Fear of freezing to death drove me to keep moving during the Antarctica Marathon, not the love of running.

Running to Leadership

Long Jump Crisis

In high school, I was a long jumper. Initially, my longest jump was around 15 feet. At a track meet, I was shocked as I stared down a rival high school's long jump runway. My high school's take off board was about 3 feet from our long sand pit. This board was about 16 feet from the short sand pit!!!

I watched in horror as a fellow jumper sprinted down the runway, took off from the board, came up short, landed very hard on the runway surface, and tumbled into the sand pit. I was too scared to take a practice jump. All I could think about injuring myself and coming up with an excuse for not jumping.

When my name was called, I was still scared. I ran down the runway, took off, extended myself in mid air, and blacked out. Much to my surprise, I landed in the pit. I had obviously fouled by taking a step over the board. However, I turned around and saw a white flag waving. It was a fair jump!!!

It measured over 18 feet. From that day forward, I consistently jumped over 18 feet. Fear of hitting the runway inspired me to dramatically improve that day, not the love of long jumping.

Running to Leadership

Facing FEARS During the Great Wall Marathon

FEARS is an acronym for a

Failure to
Evaluate
All
Reasonable
Solutions

When faced with an obstacle, I try to identify numerous solutions. The more solutions that are identified, the more comfortable I feel.

Cold fingers were my major concern at the Antarctica Marathon. My fears were mitigated after researching different gloves and mittens. I tried ones made with special materials.

Battery-powered, chemically warmed, and "breath" warmed ones were tested. Combinations of wearing gloves in mittens with mitten covers were examined. My fear didn't go away until the problem was resolved.

Running to Leadership

The Great Wall Of China Marathon's 3,600 Steps of Fear

A couple of days before the Great Wall of China Marathon, we were required to take a walking tour over part of the course. It was the 3-mile section that was actually on The Great Wall. The marathoners ran over this section twice starting around miles 3 and 20.

The Wall was built to go over the steepest hills with the steepest drop offs. After all, it's much harder to attack The Wall while running up a steep hill. Thus, running on The Wall was very challenging.

We started the tour on the rebuilt section. The marathoners had to go up and down about 3,600 steps.

Running to Leadership

This was unlike running on football stadium steps. These steps weren't the same height. Thus, it was very difficult to establish a rhythm. The Wall was not built to OSHA standards!!!

I told myself that I could live with these mild inconveniences. After all, if this were meant to be an easy race, they would not have referred to it as an "adventure" marathon. After about a mile on the rebuilt section, we came to one of the original sections of The Wall. It was here that my initial excitement soon turned to horror.

The Wall's path was about five-feet wide. Since there weren't any handrails, we didn't have much to grab, other than another person, in case we fell. There was a short wall on one side and nothing to prevent us from falling off of the other side.

The 50-foot drop offs could easily kill us. The rocks were crumbling and smooth. If it rained, we could easily slip and fall. Unfortunately, as the runners were lining up to slowly walk across this section, I was right in front of a chattering adolescent.

She asked her parents every question that I didn't want to hear.

Running to Leadership

- Has anyone died from falling off The Wall?
- How far is that drop?
- Is that far enough to kill you?
- How will they get your body? With a helicopter?
- Will it rain on Saturday?
- How slippery will these rocks get if it rains?
- Will they cancel the race?
- What do you grab to stop you from falling?
- Do you think you could grab a tree limb to keep from falling?
- Is it too late to turn around and go back?

I was very deep in thought on the bus ride back to our hotel. I was scared. I finally decided that I didn't come this far to back out. A race or life without risk is not an adventure. Or as the sign along the course read, "A race without hills is like coffee without caffeine." This was going to be a real adventure.

> *"Decide that you want it more than you're afraid of it."*
>
> – Bill Cosby

The only way for me to survive the race was to face my fears and to develop an action plan. I decided to take a lesson from drivers' education. During the treacherous sections of The Wall I would not focus on the people who were behind me. I would not let them influence or pressure me to go faster. I would go at my own, comfortable pace.

I would also maintain a five-foot gap or "safety zone" with the person in front of me. If they fell, they couldn't take me down with them.

I broke up The Wall into smaller, more manageable tasks. The roomy guard towers became my focal points and rest stops. The faster runners would pass me in the towers.

Also, since hydration was critical, I would drink water while in the towers. If I became dehydrated, I might lose my focus and slip on the stairs. The views from the towers allowed me to savor my past success and look forward to my next adventure.

I wouldn't care about my finishing time. However, the marathon had an eight-hour time limit. This was manageable. My mission was to run a marathon on every continent. It was not to finish the marathons by a certain time or to die in the process. Thus, sanity and risk mitigation prevailed in my planning.

After about seven and a half hours, I crossed the finish line. This was my slowest marathon by almost two hours. However, I didn't care. The Wall was conquered. Later that night, I was looking at the 100 photos from the marathon. It occurred to me that I stopped running for about 60 to 90 seconds to take each photo!!!

The Comfort Zone

Right now, you're probably in your comfort zone. There must be a drastic change or challenge to move you from it. The question that you have to answer is: "What role or responsibility do you want to have in managing the change?" In other words, do you want people to force you to drastically change? Or, do you want to plan, control, and implement this drastic change yourself?

All of us have comfort zones. There's nothing wrong with having one. Some people have very small comfort zones. For example, I had a relative who was practically born and raised in the same house. She raised her children, and ultimately, retired there. She never learned to drive and rarely left her hometown. She was very content in her very small comfort zone.

However, the wider your comfort zone, the more you can experience and achieve. You create more space to work in. You tend to show less fear and more curiosity. In order to widen your zone, you must move outside of it and establish a new outer boundary.

This move causes stress and pain and also exposes your weaknesses. You must face your weaknesses and flaws to develop plans to address them via the FEARS acronym.

Running to Leadership

CPA Test-Taking Crisis

After ten years of being out of college, I returned to pursue an accounting master's degree in the evenings. I was the oldest person in most of my classes. As an information technology manager, I was clearly outside of my comfort zone.

Many people had said that information technology professionals didn't understand accounting. Furthermore, I didn't have any role models. If anything, IT and accounting professionals were more adversaries than friends. During my studies, I maintained a very high GPA and was accepted into the National Accounting Honor Society.

After graduation, I began preparing for the 3.5-day Certified Public Accounting (CPA) exam. The exam's four parts were audit, law, practice, and theory. At least 75% on all four parts was required to pass. I had to pass at least two parts during one testing session to receive any credit.

Also, a grade over 50% was required on the parts that I failed. I could retake the failed parts at a later date. Thus, if I received 100% on three parts and 49% on the fourth part, I received no credit and had to retake all four parts!!!

Running to Leadership

I took a practice CPA exam and received less than 25% on all of the parts. I was devastated. I studied even harder, took another practice exam, and didn't improve. If I wanted to pass, I had to re-examine and revise my studying and test-taking strategies and techniques.

First, I realized that I was repeatedly studying the same topics. These were my favorites and I thoroughly understood them. They represented my comfort zone. However, based on the test results, my favorites only accounted for about 25% of the test. Since there were five options for each question, I was doing slightly better than guessing chances of 20%.

I needed to move out of my comfort zone and study my least favorite topics: income taxes, consolidations and eliminations, and pension accounting, to name a few. This was the only way for me to pass.

> *"It is impossible for a people to rise above their aspirations. If we think we cannot, we almost certainly cannot. Our greatest enemy is our defeatist attitude."*
>
> – Robert Williams

Unfortunately, most of us have a habit of focusing on our strengths and avoiding our weaknesses. In order to get ahead, we must move outside of our comfort zones. I forced myself to become as comfortable and proficient with my least favorite topics as my favorite ones. I actually forced myself to stop reverting back to studying my favorite topics.

My next problem was test taking. I hate taking multiple-choice tests. They have an impersonal way of telling me what I don't know—and like most people; I want to feel that I know everything. The CPA exam had hundreds of five-part multiple-choice questions.

I had to overcome my test taking fear and anxiety. I approached each of the five choices as five individual true/false questions. I also forced myself to breathe between each question. This prevented me from unconsciously holding my breath during a stressful situation and losing focus. It's hard to concentrate if your brain is short on oxygen.

I received my CPA license thanks to acknowledging my weaknesses and anxieties and developing plans to overcome them: FEARS.

Several years later, I found myself teaching all of my pre-CPA problem areas in collegiate accounting classes. I had to employ this same studying and test-taking strategies while preparing for the Project Management Professional certification.

Running to Leadership

Other People's Comfort Zones For You

Some people don't want to move outside of their personal comfort zones. In some cases, other people don't want you move outside of the comfort zone that THEY'VE established for YOU. They've put you in a box. How many of your co-workers, friends, or relatives have told you that you couldn't do something?

When you achieved the unexpected, it forced them to re-evaluate their perceptions (or prejudices). Think about it. When you did the unexpected, the strongest naysayers felt uncomfortable. It may have shaken their fundamental beliefs about people like you.

After getting suspended, my efforts were refocused on getting back into college and graduating. Once back into college, my GPA had dramatically improved. My senior advisor asked me about my post-graduation plans. I told her that I wanted an MBA.

She looked at me and said that she didn't think that I was "grad school material" and probably won't get admitted. I was shocked to hear this from a person who was supposed to be supportive of my goals.

I calmly explained that I had been offered academic scholarships and graduate teaching assistantships from two of the top MBA programs. I was also accepted into a Ph.D. program in mathematics. My advisor promptly walked out.

She had very low expectations of me. Her comfort zone for me was a very small comfort zone. She also

felt uncomfortable that I had challenged her perceptions. Her comfort zones for me didn't prevent me
achieving academic successes.

Subsequently, I earned two graduate degrees and
three highly sought after professional certifications; a
certificate as a Project Management Professional,
Supply Chain Manager, and Certified Public Accoun-
tant (CPA).

> *"Unless we start to believe in ourselves, we will never
> convince anyone to believe in us. It is time to believe
> in ourselves."*
>
> **-** Ronald H. Brown

The "Opposite" Mind Trap

Part of moving out of your comfort zone involves
changing your mindset. We may start with something
as simple our understanding of opposites. We're
taught to believe that that you're either a scholar or an
athlete; a technical person or a business person; left
handed or right handed. This mindset has forced
some people to believe that they can't cross over the
barrier to the opposite side without a great many sa-
crifices.

However, when we step back and look at the big picture, we see that opposites are really the same thing
and they must co-exist. One cannot exist without the

other. For example, you can't have an "off" without its related "on."

Think about what happened when someone thought out of the box. They invented the variable dimmer switch. The dimmer focuses on the amount of lightness (or darkness) in small increments. A traditional light switch focuses on the extremes.

This old mindset has prevented athletes from becoming scholars and, conversely, scholars from becoming athletes. When many people see my academic credentials (four degrees), they see a nerd or geek. They visualize an uncoordinated, thick eye-glass wearing, unfit individual. This represents their comfort zone.

They become overwhelmed when they learned about my athletic accomplishments.

- Earned high school letters in track and soccer
- Completed a 100-mile bicycle race
- Completed over ninety 26.2-mile marathons, including winning awards
- Completed marathons on all seven continents, including Antarctica
- Earned a brown belt in karate

I have refused to limit my goals based on other people's low expectations and perceptions. Over the years, I've talked with parents who have seen their smart and bright junior and high students "dummy down" to be with their peers.

Their peers felt that you couldn't be a rap artist, have boyfriends, or be an athlete while being intelligent. Yet, these intelligent people (i.e. doctors, lawyers, accountants, etc.) are the very ones that they'll rely on when they graduate from high school.

Some other deterrents to self-motivation are the various career and success indicators. These are the tests that students take that help determine what career they should pursue. The counterparts, in the business world, are the tests that supposedly predict your success as a manager or executive.

If you truly believe you can be successful in a different field, you should pursue it. Rather than to accept the results of the test as final, think of them as identifying possible weaknesses for you to improve upon.

For example, a career test revealed that I should be in a highly analytical field, such as math or engineering. My math grades also supported the test results. However, I enjoyed sports, writing, public speaking, and art—the "soft" skills.

My professional positions were in the highly analytical fields of computers and accounting. However, I worked equally hard on improving my "soft" skills. I took classes and associated with professionals in those areas.

Subsequently, I became a successful athlete, writer, professional speaker, and photographer. I also served on the board of director for a professional theatrical organization and co-founded a national running organization. All the while, I was still highly analytical.

"I Tried" Trophy

I took five steps forward down the hallway. The hallway was outside of the restrooms. During those steps, I pushed the ball out, swung it back, swung it forward, released it, and followed through. All these actions were done with complete control and consistency. This was how Mr. Chisom taught me to bowl at the Ringside Bowl Lanes in St. Louis, MO.

I was about six years old and could barely lift the ball, let alone control it. It was a real struggle. When I was on the actual bowling lanes, I was the Gutter Ball King. Despite my lack of talent (and score), every Saturday morning my brother and I showed up.

At the end of the season, they awarded me the first ever "I Tried" trophy. My average was 63. Regardless of the number of gutter balls I had thrown, I never gave up. By the time I was a teenager, I had made it to the finals of the citywide youth bowling tournament.

The funny thing about bowling is that you have to be consistent on your first ball. All ten pins are standing in fixed locations. You usually stand in the same place each time and repeat the same motion for the strike.

However, you have a great deal of flexibility on your second ball to pick up the spare. You change your starting location depending on the pin arrangement. I thrived in this structured, yet flexible environment of bowling.

Today, I find myself reliving and recapturing this "I Tried" spirit. The more gutters I threw, the closer I would get to a strike. It didn't matter how many times I failed. I kept forging ahead with that childlike, "I'll master this thing" mentality. I'd study my mistakes, make an adjustment, and try again.

I've seen this same drive with children trying to master making free throws. They'll stay up past daylight to shoot baskets outside well into the night. I sometimes wonder if as adults, we've developed a "can't do" attitude. This keeps us from trying after a few failures, while children just simply don't know when to stop.

Take a few minutes and think about your fondest childhood memory of overcoming an obstacle. It may have been learning to ride a bicycle, swimming the length of a pool, or running a non-stop lap around a track. Try to recapture that feeling to motivate you as you execute your plan.

"Too many people are afraid to look deep down and see where they made mistakes. You have to take an honest look and have an honest evaluation of your performance."

– Tiger Woods
USA Today, March 26, 2007

Running to Leadership

Leading from Behind

One of my favorite small marathons was the Dallas Trails Marathon. It was one of the few marathons with a weight division. Since I weigh over 200 pounds, I enjoyed racing in this division. Over the years, I won five trophies in my weight class.

The race started on the hill near Winfred Point at Dallas' White Rock Lake. It headed east, past the Botanical Garden, towards Garland Road. At Mockingbird, it heads up the Dallas Trail towards LBJ Freeway. After reaching the halfway point, we retrace the route back to Winfred Point. However, instead of finishing by making a right turn to run back up the hill, the runners veer towards the left and go around the base of the hill. Thus, the finish line is hidden from view.

One year, I was trying to catch a runner near the end of the race. He approached the fork in the road and came to a complete stop. He didn't see the finish line, which was around the hill, and didn't know which way to go. He saw runners on the hilltop. However, they offered no assistance.

I was faced with a decision. Do I

1. Say nothing, run past him, and hope to finish in front of him?
2. Tell him to turn right (i.e the wrong direction) and go up the hill?
3. Tell him to veer left and finish in front of me?

Running to Leadership

I yelled for him to veer to the left. He finished ahead of me by about 100 yards.

One of my staff members was an amateur race car driver. He described a good manager to me in racing terms. A good manager gives his team the best available racecars (i.e. the best tools); instructs the team to drive the cars as fast as they desired (i.e. makes decisions); and is responsible for removing all of the road bumps and for manning the pit crews.

In other words, my role was to let my staff do what they do best, whether that was to design databases, write programs, or analyze business requirements. I wasn't going to micro-manage them. I supplied  them with the best available tools and resolved any conflicts that arose. They drove the fast, shiny cars; I worked in the background. I led them from behind.

My staff had completed a major multi-year, international project in January. I was so confident that they would finish on time that, a year earlier, I had scheduled a two-week, non-refundable vacation for February.

One of my staff members was the star of the company's February quarterly meeting as he proudly gave the project's final report. In the meantime, I was departing from Argentina and sailing to Antarctica. Since he drove the race car, it was fitting for him to be in the "winner's circle."

Running to Leadership

A Little Change Adds Up

Change is both a noun and a verb. When I run, I look for change on the ground. When I return home, I put it in an orange plastic Gatorade jar. It used to hold the powered mix. Over time, the jar has accumulated between $35 and $50 in change.

When I was around eight years old, I was rushed to the hospital. After a couple of days there, the doctors told me I would become a diabetic by the time I was a teenager. I would have to give myself daily insulin injections. This was on my mind constantly all through my high school years.

My high school made it mandatory for all students to participate in an organized sport for a minimum of two out of the three seasons, and during your off season, you had to take physical education. I ran cross-country for a couple of seasons, played soccer in the cold St. Louis winters, and ran track in the spring.

My track talents limited me to being the fifth man on a four-man relay team. That is to say, I was better than the average person, but not good enough for a college team. However, I lost weight and didn't have to take insulin.

During this same period, I worked as a waiter and dishwasher in a barbeque restaurant. One of the cooks was a diabetic who lost his eye due to glaucoma. Later, his toes and then one of his legs were amputated due to diabetes. Finally, he lost his life due to complications with the disease. This scared me.

In college, I read *Aerobics* and *New Aerobics* by Dr. Kenneth Cooper. He wrote that diabetics who were dependent on insulin decreased or completely went off of insulin as a result of maintaining a simple fitness program. I decided to adopt a life-time fitness program. I planned to average running three miles or about thirty minutes a day to avoid taking insulin.

As of December 31, 2010, I had logged 35,015 miles of running and averaged 3.31 miles a day – and I've never taken any medications for diabetes. This lead to my book, *Running Shoes are Cheaper than Insulin: Marathon Adventures on All Seven Continents*.

A little bit of change adds up.

Change is very difficult for some people. Unfortunately, in order for businesses to be competitive in today's global economy, they must be prepared to be in a constant state of flux. Managers must become the cheerleaders for change: they have to motivate their employees to change.

Also, employees must constantly change themselves, if they want to remain marketable. This means learning new technologies and processes. These things may have to be learned outside of the workplace on the employee's personal time, which can be daunting.

Running to Leadership

Change under stressful situations is very challenging. I was a project manager at the now defunct Superconducting Super Collider (SSC) Project. It was an exciting place to work. I was responsible for selecting and implementing the accounting-related applications. This included payables, receivables, fixed assets, the general ledger, procurement, and other applications, as well as the technical infrastructure used to support them.

During the early phases of the project, Congress was deciding whether or not to continue funding the SSC. Imagine working for an organization that may not be around in a year or eighteen months. Morale was down and some people started to leave.

This problem was compounded by working with a new technology that had a bad track record for implementation failures. It had previously taken twenty-four to twenty-seven months to be fully implemented. My project plan was for only nine months. Also, Congressional committees had sent representatives down to investigate how we were doing, so any little mistake could have ended up on the front page of a major newspaper or magazine.

Key members of the project team went through a simple "change analysis" exercise. It was the same logic that I used to avoid insulin by running. They took a sheet of paper and drew a line down the middle. One the left side, they each listed all the bad things that would happen if the project failed.

Running to Leadership

They listed things like,

- √ I could lose my job.
- √ I may not get a raise.
- √ I may not get a promotion.
- √ I may not be able to pay my bills.

On the right side of the page, they listed what good things might happen if the project succeeded:

- √ I may keep my job.
- √ I may get a raise.
- √ I may get a bonus.
- √ Even if I lose my job, I'll still be more marketable with my new skills.

This list was very personal. It had nothing to do with what would happen to the SSC. Each team member had to have a personal, selfish motive for why they wanted to succeed. They reminded themselves of these reasons throughout the project.

We successfully implemented the applications within nine months. Later, Congress voted to kill the SSC project on a Thursday evening, and the news was all over the TV stations in Dallas. The next day, I walked into my office to find I had messages from all around the country from people who wanted to hire my staff. Within a couple of months, everyone had a job offer in hand. And the offers were more than their current salaries.

Running to Leadership

Crabs & Geese

After I was kicked out of college, I found work as a computer operator. My co-workers were college dropouts and people who had never attended college. One evening, I was printing payroll checks, and I was stunned at the high salaries for people with degrees. So I got back into college after missing a couple of semesters.

I worked the graveyard shift from about 11 p.m. until 8 a.m. During the slow periods, we would shoot the breeze or read magazines and comic books, and have pity parties about our college failures.

A pity party is when a group of people support one another in their failures. In fact, they actually encourage one another not to try to succeed. For example, we were making "good money," and we didn't have to lift heavy boxes like day laborers or work at construction jobs. We didn't need more money. We were happy.

The pity party ended when I returned to college. Instead of reading comic books during the downtimes, I'd study. One morning, my non-degreed boss fired me. He claimed that I had been late too many times.

 I was stunned by the accusation. I realized that the pity partiers were like crabs in a barrel. If any of them attempted to climb out of the barrel, the others would pull it back down. I

had to keep my ambitions to myself.

My trip to run the Great Wall of China Marathon was full of fun and excitement. It was the first time that I had been on an organized guided tour as an adult. This was also the first time that I had been with a bunch of marathoners from around the world in close quarters. When I returned to the office, I was on cloud nine. However, my excitement quickly turned to unexplained depression, which lasted for several weeks.

About a year later, I was on a ship going to run the Antarctica Marathon. The ship held about 125 people, including the staff. Again, I would be surrounded by distance runners and their understanding supporters for about ten days. My evenings were spent in the ship's lounge area, where I'd transfer photos from my camera to my laptop, delete and edit the photos, and update my journal.

One evening, a Canadian shipmate observed me working and struck up a conversation. He explained that he wasn't a distance runner. In fact, he was a chain smoker and non-athlete. He had come on the trip to support a friend.

He went on to say that after years of trying to quit smoking, he had managed to do it on the trip. He described being on board with the runners was like being at religious revival. The one exception was that there wasn't a preacher or choir "whipping us up into a frenzy."

Running to Leadership

Everyone was so highly self-motivated and self-confident that it was highly contagious. We were our own evangelists. He completely lost his urge and desire to smoke. He felt one hundred percent supported by the group, without even having asked for their support.

Nobody questioned his ability or desire to stop smoking. Anything that you wanted to do, everyone would support you and try to help you, either personally or using their contacts. It didn't matter if you wanted to climb Mt. Everest or start your own business.

These distance runners were like the geese, that I encountered while running at Dallas' White Rock Lake. During the late fall and into the early winter, geese migrate to the lake for the winter.

They fly in their V-formation, with the lead goose doing most of the work while the others draft off of one another. They honk to offer encouragement to one another. If a goose gets sick along the way, a couple of geese will remain with him until he gets better. Then they will fly together, as a team, to catch up with the main flock.

Thus, when selecting members for a project team, I worked very hard at keeping the crabs away. I'd much rather have a less experienced, yet eager, team member, than a crab, who would bring the morale down and cause the project to fail.

I learned to surround myself with geese, the people who'll support me, and to get rid of the crabs.

The Third I – Instructions (Planning)

> ## *"People don't plan to fail. They fail to plan."*
>
> ## - Unknown

How Planning Entered the Equation

I've planned and managed projects for almost 30 years. Eventually, I earned my Project Management Professional (PMP) certification.

As I talked with highly successful people, I noticed that they were planners. It didn't matter if they were climbing Mt. Everest, running a marathon, leading troops into battle, or heading a global, multi-million dollar company. They were all great planners and it was almost second-nature to them.

70

Running to Leadership

Events just didn't "happen." They were well thought out in advance. They successfully translated their SMART goal (or vision) into a project plan. And they motivated people to follow the plan. A good plan consists of more than writing the tasks. You must identify the:

- dependencies between the tasks
- estimated durations
- tasks' start and finish dates, and
- resources used to complete the tasks

The resources are people, money, or materials. If you have small children, a babysitter might be one of your resources. Most plans fail because something was missing, such as a task or resource. It's important for someone who has achieved the goal, to review your plan for thoroughness. Achievers enjoy helping others by sharing their experiences with novices.

Planning Problems

Three major problems associated with planning are

1. Failure to manage risks – Bad things can happen with any plan. We can run out of money. A major resource won't be available. We made need more resources than originally thought. These are things that we may have been aware of during the planning stage, but didn't include in the plan.

2. Analysis paralysis – We spend so much time planning, that we never execute the plan. This is almost

the opposite of failure to plan for risks. This is the "never ending" planning cycle.

3. Failure to gain support – As your plan is executed, you may find that your resources aren't helping you. Furthermore, they don't understand why you're angry with them.

We'll examine each of these problems more closely.

"If you can somehow think and dream about success in small steps, every time you make a step, every time you accomplish a small goal, it gives you confidence to go on from there."

- John H. Johnson

Managing Risk & The Missing Worker

A Mt. Everest climber said, "The person with the most recovery plans wins." This logic is supported by good project planning.

When some people develop plans, they assume that everything will go smoothly. However, reality tells us that this isn't always the case. Our failure to recognize and address the potential trouble spots can be very costly.

Running to Leadership

When contingency plans are constructed for potential problems, the probability for success increases. In project planning, this is referred to as risk mitigation and management. You identify the:

- potential problem or risk
- probability of the event occurring
- events that may forewarn that the problem is about to occur
- cost of correcting the problem, if it occurs
- corrective action you plan to take
- individual responsible for monitoring the problem and implementing the corrective action

A good contingency plan reduces the anxiety of dealing with unwanted changes.

The Missing Worker

After developing the plan for a large multi-million dollar, international project, we asked, "Based on the past projects, what are your concerns?" People leaving before the project's completion was their biggest concern. They could have a:

- major medical problem, such as a heart attack
- better job offer from another company
- get hit by a train
- retire

We couldn't guarantee that none of these events would occur. However, we tried to ensure that all the tasks were in the plan, resources were assigned to the tasks, all of the critical tasks were well documented, and everyone had a backup person who could step in, if needed.

A couple of weeks before the implementation date, a key team member went missing. A couple of days passed before his wife called. He was being held in a deportation facility. Needless to say, he wasn't returning to the office.

Our VP ran into my office about the unplanned departure. He thought that the project would certainly fail or be delayed. I explained we had executed the "AWOL" contingency plan. We replaced his name in our plan with that of his pre-assigned backup. Our deadline was unchanged. The project was implemented on time, under budget, and to specifications.

> *"The guy who takes a chance, who walks the line between the known and unknown, who is unafraid of failure, will succeed."*
>
> - Gordon Parks

Cheetahs on the Safaricom Lewa Marathon Course

Before Kenya's Safaricom Lewa Marathon, we went on photo safaris. It gave us opportunities to see the course. The marathon was held in the Lewa Wildlife Conservancy. We ran twice around a 13.1-mile loop.

Running to Leadership

As we drove along the dirt road, we were surrounded by fields of tall grasses and mountains, instead of parking lots and buildings. This also meant that were would be almost no cheering crowds and very little shade to block the sun. As it turned out, these were the least of my worries. The animals would be roaming freely during the race!!!

As we rode over a hill, we spotted a couple of rhinos. Our driver and guide told us about the rhino's weight, speed, and temper. We quickly determined that they could outrun us.

We asked the obvious questions.

Q1. What should we do if we encounter a rhino during the marathon?
A1. Stand still and slowly walk backwards.
Q2. What should we do if a rhino charges us?
A2. Zigzag. They're terrible at turning corners.

I made a mental note to conserve my energy in case I had to run sprints. I just hoped that I would be sprinting towards the finish line instead of away from it. At least rhinos aren't predators—which was one good thing at least. They don't hunt and eat people. That was a big relief.

Over the next hill, we spotted three cheetahs. They were walking on the course and looking at the course directional signs. This was a little nerve racking. The guide explained that the cheetahs may be brothers. They were very strong and fast, hunt as a single unit, and can quickly bring down a zebra.

As we watched the cheetahs looking at the course and looking back at us, we felt that it wasn't worth asking the same questions about the cheetahs that we'd asked about the rhinos. Once a cheetah looked at us on the course, we felt that we couldn't outrun it and might even zigzag right into one of the other two.

So instead we asked, "How often do they eat?" He explained that a zebra will last the trio about three or four days. As we rode over the next hill, we found a zebra herd. We hoped that one would be missing tonight.

On the eve of the race, the runners were apprehensively talking about race day. Most of us had seen episodes of the *Wild Kingdom* and *National Geographic*. We nervously joked that predators go after the old, very young, solitary, and/or injured animals.

So, it was important not to be the slowest in the group, run alone, or limp!!! We identified the risk and had a plan. All of us managed to finish the race without any problems.

"Analysis paralysis manifests itself through exceedingly long phases of project planning, requirements gathering, program design and modeling, with little or no extra value created by those steps."

Source: Wikipedia, the Free Encyclopedia

Running to Leadership

Analysis Paralysis

"Analysis paralysis" can be a major problem with the planning process. This occurs when a person becomes so entangled in the planning that the plan never gets executed. This was my major problem. I can always find something wrong or a good reason not to proceed. There were several reasons behind my "analysis paralysis."

- I knew too much. - The more you know, the more reasons you can find for a plan to fail.
- I'm afraid of failure or risk-taking. - Why should I risk moving outside of my comfort zone? After all, my comfort zone is nice and warm.
- I can't depend on other people. - "They" are the reasons that projects fail and I don't control "them."

I could spend years developing the perfect plan and miss thousands of opportunities along the way. At some point, I had to accept the unknown problems, deal with the risks and execute the plan. I surrounded myself with reliable people and executed the plan.

We realized that we rarely had all of the information that was needed to completely develop and execute the plan. So, we actually built the task of "re-planning" into the project plan. In large projects, many decisions can't be made until the analysis is complete. This leaves many TBD (to be determined) tasks.

These tasks are documented and expounded throughout the project. Thus, the plan was a living organism which grew throughout the project.

Gaining Support From Your Resources

A resource is anything that you need to accomplish your goal. This includes people, money, and materials. When putting together your plan, it's always important to identify all of your resources.

My wife defined a resource as a

REliable SOURCE

An unreliable resource must be offset with one or more reliable backups. For example, your primary babysitter choice may be a "no cost" parent. However, if the parent is unreliable, a drop off daycare facility or alternate babysitter may be your back-ups. However, an additional resource (i.e. money) may be required.

> *"A lack of planning on your part doesn't constitute an emergency on my part."*
>
> -Unknown

People Resources

Many projects fail because the people resources weren't aware that they were a part of the project. This also implies that they were not involved in developing the plan.

Frequently, it's assumed that the resources are available or supportive while the plan is developed. How many times were you "volunteered" for a project and you were never asked about your current assignments? Or you were asked to support a project without having any input?

You felt like your opinion was insignificant. Also, you either had to drop or delay an existing project or reassign it to someone else. You felt that you were constantly fighting fires and never saw a project through to completion.

To combat this problem, after you've completed your plan, you should print it out. Needless to say, this implies that the plan is in writing. It should include at a minimum:

- Tasks
- Durations
- Start Date
- End Date
- Predecessors
- Comments
- Resources (People, Money, and Materials)

It's important to review your plan with your resources prior to executing it. You'll need their approval. If this is a plan to achieve a personal goal, your resources may be surprised that you actually have a printed plan with their name on it. (Seeing their name on a plan is good for their ego.) For the most part, many people have never seen a printed, personal project plan.

As your resource reviews your plan, they'll probably offer tips and suggestions. They may be so impressed that you actually have a written plan that they'll provide more resources than you requested. They'll realize that you mean business and plan to succeed. Everyone wants to be a part of a winning team and consistent winners always have a plan.

Monetary Resources

Most plans need money. It's not unusual for financial problems to occur during the project. Funds were redirected from my projects to more critical corporate problems. Once, I lost my tuition reimbursement benefits when I changed jobs and had to pay for my classes.

When creating the plan, identify all of your financial requirements. If it's to pursue a degree in the evening, your costs should not only include tuition, but books, dinner or snacks, additional gasoline, tutors, internet access, laptop, babysitters, and software.

Talk with other people who have accomplished the goal and learn about their expenses. As you review your plan with your resources, ask them about any expenses that you may have omitted. They may be so impressed with your plan that they may offer to fund the project. Also, as you developed your risk mitigation plan, you should include those costs into your budget.

Your back-up financial resources may be your savings accounts, loans against your 401K, credit card cash advances, bank or credit union loans, or monies from family members. In any case, it's important to identify these financial resources, and in some cases, get pre-approved before you begin your project. The time it takes to begin the process of obtaining financial resources "in the heat of the project battle" may spell defeat for your plan.

It's important to budget for a celebration or "thank you" event for your resources. It could be something a simple as a lunch, some flowers, or a thank you card. Or it could be as elaborate as a family cruise.

Material Resources

Material resources are the things that you'll actually need to complete your plan. These could be anything from running shoes, jelly beans, and electrolytes for marathons, to study guides for certification exams.

Running to Leadership

Project Plan Review Process

Once the plan is com-
pleted, it must be re-
viewed by your resources
and support team. Hope-
fully, at least one of them
has previously achieved
your goal. You may draw
from their personal expe-
rience to provide additional advice. Also, consider
looking for plans on the Internet.

Due to the length of most plans, schedule an initial
meeting with the reviewer to go over the high points.
Instruct them to focus on the missing tasks, dependencies, and resources. Ask them about any problems that they encountered while reaching the goal.
Encourage them to be critical.

Let them know that you value their time and will schedule a follow-up meeting. This gives them a chance to
contemplate their previous experiences and to en-
hance your plan. During the follow-up meeting, listen
to their concerns, make the appropriate modifications,
and thank them for their time.

Skimping on Support & Talent

Novice runners initially ask questions about running
shoes. Some of them are stunned at their cost.

Running to Leadership

They're especially, surprised to learn that I have to get another pair every couple of months.

I explain that I spend less per day on my shoes, than they spend on their daily coffee and soda. These same people will spend more money on fancy shoes and wear them only a few miles.

Distance runners quickly learn that your feet are critical to your success. If you take care of them, they'll take care of you. They support your entire body. If they're out of line, it may impact your skeletal system. And this system supports your spine. If your spine isn't well support or is out of line, it may affect the rest of your body and lead to depression.

So, I strongly encourage people to spend their money and pay attention to their basic, fundamental support. In business, this is your people.

One corporation decided to establish a low bid policy for selecting consultants. They felt that they would save money by using lower priced workers. Unfortunately, they didn't understand the job market or basic human logic.

When we needed a consultant, our procurement department would contact the suppliers, i.e. consulting firms. The firms responded with their lowest possible rates and resumes of available consultants.

Running to Leadership

Our procurement department was amazed at the low rates and quality of the resumes. However, there were two fundamental problems.

First, by the time we completed the request for quote process, the candidate may not be available. Second, if this great candidate is available, then "Why?"

One of my staff members almost exclusively used consultants. His small staff was like a revolving door. His consultants lasted about three to four weeks. And he was back into the multi-week cycle to find a replacement. Thus, his projects were almost always late.

The problem was simple. We didn't pay people what they were really worth. The consultant firms didn't have a staff of internal (Form W2) consultants, who were getting paid while they were waiting on projects. Instead, they had a stockpile of resumes of potential, independent (Form 1099) consultants.

The independent consultants were like professional gunslingers or mercenaries. They didn't have any allegiance to the consulting firm or our corporation. They went to the highest paying contract offer.

Thus, if they were between jobs, they would take anything (i.e. work for us) until a better offer came along. And since we were paying well below market, almost ever offer was higher. For example, earning an extra $10 to $20 an hour more translated to $400 to $800 per week more.

Running to Leadership

The consultants weren't worried the short time period on their resume, which they spent with us. They simply left the time period blank, said they were on vacation, and didn't use us as a reference.

After several late projects, we were able to quantify the cost to the business for their lateness and showed a positive ROI for paying more for the consultants in order to reduce turnover.

Skimping on support, doesn't always save money.

The Balancing Acts

Training for a marathon requires months of preparation. There are hundreds of different training programs for people to follow. These are based on various criteria, such as previous running or walking experience and/or projected finishing time. Most of these programs are built on 4 techniques or phases.

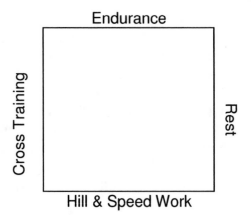

Running to Leadership

Your weekly training is divided into three or four days of running, one day of rest, and two or three days of aerobic cross training. Cross training may consists of biking, swimming, walking, elliptical machines, or aerobic fitness classes. These activities may last from thirty to sixty minutes.

The endurance phase is used to build your core base mileage. You gradually increase your long runs to about fifteen miles. Your other weekly runs may increase to 6 to 9 miles each day.

After your long run reaches between twelve to fifteen miles, you substitute one of your shorter weekday runs for training on hills. You find a "nice" short hill and begin running repetitions.

Over time, you increase the number of repetitions and/or increase the length or steepness of the hills. This mentally prepares you for the hills during the marathon.

During this time period, your long runs are gradually increasing to between eighteen and twenty-one miles.

Following several weeks of hill training, you swap the hill training for speed work. This is usually done on a track or marked off course. The focus is on getting faster, without getting injured. Like doing the hill training, the number of laps is gradually increased and/or your times are gradually decreasing.

Running to Leadership

The final pillar in the training program is rest. The further along you go in the program, the more susceptible you are to injury. Thus, it's important to closely monitor yourself and your workouts. Resting gives your body a chance to recover.

It's possible to finish a marathon without adhering to these four training concepts. However, you may not reach your time-related goal. About one-third of runners, who train for their first marathon, never make it to the starting line due to injuries. However, managing this delicate balance, along with self monitoring, leads to success.

This four-prong approach to marathon training is also applicable to managing successful projects. Failure to pay attention any one of the four criteria, could easily led to a project's failure.

As a project manager, it was my responsibility to develop a balanced project schedule. I developed the schedule to utilize all of the resources to deliver a quality product by a certain date.

Unfortunately, it's difficult for some people to fully understand the relationship between changing the scope and the other constraints.

When the scope is increased, the other three constraints are directly affected. More resources may be needed to complete the project. Resources are people, money, and materials. If more resources are not added, then the time frame might be increased to accommodate the additional workload. And more testing may be required to ensure that the product functions correctly with the additional requirements.

If the time, resources, and quality are not adjusted with the additional business requirements, the project may fail either while it's being developed or become costly to maintain after it's completed. As the saying goes, "There's never enough time to do it right the first time, but there's always enough time to fix it later."

To help illustrate this point to the project team and executives, you'll need a square floor tile (or one square foot sheet of glass), a rock, and a marker. Using the marker, write Scope, Resources, Quality, and Time on the floor tile.

Now, write "Scope Change" on the rock.

During the meeting,

1. Explain that the tile represents your balanced project schedule. The project's scope can be completed in the time frame, with the agreed upon resources, at an acceptable level of quality.
2. Balance the tile on your finger to illustrate the point.
3. Take the "Scope Change" rock and place it on the side of the tile marked "Scope."
4. After everything falls on the floor, tell them that this is what happens when a scope request is accepted, that doesn't account for changes in resources, time, or quality.
5. You want every scope change to come packaged with the resources, time, and quality to make the project successful. If not, the project may crash.

Both the project schedule and marathon training schedule must be balanced to be successful.

Why the Scope Changes & How to Prevent Them.

The scope defines the project's goals and objectives. When autopsies (or lessons learned) were performed on projects, scope-related problems always rise to the top of the list.

I conducted a study of the root cause for software changes. The results were subsequently published in an international IT magazine. This involved analyzing software changes over an entire year.

The cause of the changes were classified into one of three categories; extra, wrong, or missing.

Running to Leadership

Extra – Something was in the software, which should not have been there. For example, a report or screen may have a column, which needed to be removed and not replaced. A report may include an incorrectly displayed social security number. The software might even contain a virus or worm.

Wrong – The software contained logic or a requirement, which was written incorrectly. Examples might include a mistyped formula, incorrect dates, or the wrong data on a report. A report may show a person's birth date, instead of their age.

Missing – Logic to perform a function was completely missing from the business requirements and, subsequently, from the software. A change request was submitted to add the functionality.

About eighty percent of the problems occurred because something was missing from the business requirements. This tells us that people are not doing a thorough job of both providing and gathering initial requirements.

Poor initial requirements gathering leads to "scope creep." Subsequently, this leads to the never ending requests to add functionality to a project after it has started. These requests are both formal and behind the scenes.

We implemented formal business requirement document reviews and structured walkthroughs. The documents were distributed before the meetings for people to review. Notes and changes were recorded during the meetings. Next, these changes were made to the scope document.

Despite this review process, the problems continued. After sitting in several of the reviews, I noticed that the facilitators asked people to see if the documents were correct. However, they failed to emphasize them to look for what was missing.

The sentence, "Jack went up the hill to fetch a pail of water." is correct. However, "and Jill" is missing. The facilitator needed be very explicit about how to read the documents and ask clarifications about the requirements.

For example, an executive wanted a new sales order system. The business requirements document indicated that the scope was limited to a sales order system.

The requirements were written by an analyst and approved by both the technical and sales management teams. However, there two different views on a sales order system.

The technical team thought this was software that accepted a sales order from the account representative and sent it to the warehouse for fulfillment.

The sales executives thought it was a system that accepted sales orders, processed sales returns, tracked the reasons that the items were returned, checked the customer credit, determined the sales force commissions, and sent the request to the warehouse and accounts payable.

This additional functionality was missing from the original requirements documents and led to scope changes throughout the project. Although this additional functionality wasn't in writing, it was required for the system to be successful.

Leading Without a Map

After years of running, I decided to spend my summer by participating in biathlons. These involved running and bicycling during the same race. Since this was relatively new, the race directors established their own policies and formats.

Some directors started with the run portion. They felt that this prevented the bicyclists from drafting and they didn't have to monitor the course as closely. Drafting is a cyclist is riding very close behind another cyclist. The cyclist in the rear benefits from the reduction in air pressure and uses less energy. Thus, the rear cyclist has more energy for the run section. In co-ed races, a male could conspire with a female. She could draft off of him and save her energy for the run.

The 1985 Mesquite Biathlon consisted of a thirteen-mile bike leg followed by a three-mile run. We were able to draft during the bicycle leg. Thus, I was able to conserve energy for the run. Much to my surprise, I found myself in the first group to finish the bicycling course. The race was going to go the fastest runner. Since I was a marathoner, I still had a lot of energy and was confident of my ability to win.

After the run started, I quickly realized that I didn't know where I was going. Therefore, I relied heavily on the course monitors to direct me. Along one stretch of the road, some of the runners yelled at me. I should have made a right turn to get to the finish line. I doubled back. However, I was unable to recover from the additional 150 yards and finished third in my age group.

Evidently, the course monitor didn't realize that I was in the race!!! He watched me run right past him and didn't say anything. Needless to say, I was upset. I felt that it was impossible for the other runners to catch me during the final stretch. However, the race director pointed out that as a participant, I have the responsibility to know the race course to avoid getting lost. Ever since this incident, I always ask for a map or a complete project plan. There's more about this lesson in "When in Doubt...Stop" on page 111.

The Fourth I – Implementation (Execution)

> **"A good plan, that's well executed, is better than an excellent plan on paper."**
>
> **General George S. Patton**

How Execution Entered the Equation

I went to the mailbox and retrieved the letter that I had been dreading. I had been placed on academic suspension. The better part of that winter break was spent blaming everyone for my personal failures.

- The teachers were too hard.
- They assigned too much homework.
- I came from a disadvantaged background.
- They didn't test me over the material that I knew.
- They didn't give me enough time to study.
- The textbooks were poorly written.
- The classes were too long.
- The professors talked too fast.
- The professors wrote too fast and erased the material before I could write it down.
- The classes were too early in the morning.

- The students weren't helpful and were snobby.
- The classes didn't relate to my major.
- My test grades didn't reflect my real knowledge of the subject matter.
- The professors didn't ask the right questions.
- Family problems had distracted me.

Over the next few months, I found plenty of people who supported my views. In other words, I had successfully developed a network of people who supported my failure. We had great "pity parties."

They were actually happy to see me fail. My failure supported and further justified their failures. I had lived up to their low expectations of me.

I blamed everyone, except me. It wasn't my fault. It was The System. I was The Victim. I was not responsible for my failures.

I spent the better part of three or four months blaming The System. Then I realized that it was my fault. The System was not going to change. I had to accept responsibility for my actions before any progress could be made. I realized that I had spent too much time going to parties and spending time with friends. I was also procrastinating.

I had to learn to make the right decisions regarding how I spent my time. My college transcript didn't have a place for my excuses. It didn't have a place to list the parties that I had attended, the friends I had made, or my expertise at games. It only had room for the semester, course numbers, names, and grades. Not excuses.

I realized that I had to work hard to reach my goals. If everyone could get a college degree, the degree would have little or no value. I also realized that earning the degree was my first test at setting and reaching long-term goals.

In elementary, middle, and high school, the legal and academic institutions set my long-term goals. They "forced" me to go to school from kindergarten through the twelfth grade. If I didn't go to school, the authorities would contact my parents, search for me, and return me to classes. Education for people younger than 18 was not optional.

However, after 18, education was optional. The colleges didn't force me to do anything. They didn't even call my parents when I failed. They didn't even call me. They didn't remind me about upcoming assignments or exams.

They provided long-term road maps (or plans) via the college catalog and the degree programs. The short-term road map was the course syllabus. I had to motivate myself to execute the plans and achieve the goals.

Running to Leadership

Hard things takes time to do. Impossible things takes a little longer

If I wanted a degree, I had to work for it. Earning a degree was my first test at goal setting, short- and long-term planning, self-motivating, and executing. This realization was a major turning point in my life.

If I wanted to succeed, it was up to me. I had to accept responsibility for my failures. I had to objectively determine the:

- reasons for my failures
- roles in my failures
- lessons learned from my mistakes
- plans for avoiding failures in the future

Just like my college transcript, there would be no place in my life to write my excuses. Successfully executing my life's plan was completely up to me.

Execution & Its Related Obstacles

The execution process is cyclical.

- You focus on completing each individual task. If your plan is well defined, each task is small and manageable.
- While executing the task, you motivate yourself and your resources. As you complete enough tasks, your resources will start motivating you to finish. They can smell a winner and they want to be a part of your winning team.
- You look at your previously completed tasks to draw your strength, self trust, self confidence, and self motivation to complete your current and future tasks.

It's important that you monitor yourself throughout the process and take appropriate breaks. And of course, celebrate when you finish.

Running to Leadership

The more you accomplish; the more personal history you have to motivate you. When running through 2,400 feet of ankle deep mud during the Antarctica Marathon, I thought about the non-stop rains during the Hartford Marathon.

As I approached the foot of the Collins Glacier, I thought about the 3,600 steps of the Great Wall of China Marathon. As the winds gusted up to 40 MPH, thoughts about the long windy stretches during the Tri-Cities Marathon came to mind. The biting cold temperatures reminded me of playing on our high school's soccer team in the cold St. Louis winters.

Running to Leadership

There are several barriers that prevent people from executing their plan to achieve their goals. Some of these barriers include:

- Dealing with dead bodies and spider love
- Managing unplanned events and stress
- Procrastinating
- Delegating

Dead Bodies & Spider Love

I was watching the late Tammy Faye Bakker-Messner on VH1's *The Surreal Life*. She was telling an audience about her experiences with making difficult and personal life-changing decisions. She used an analogy of carrying a dead body on her back. The physical weight of the body slows you down.

As the body decomposes, you get the diseases and infections from the dead body. Ultimately, the dead body can kill you. You have to make a decision. You may carry the dead body and die. Or you may cut it loose and live. The choice is yours.

Several times in my life I had found myself carrying dead bodies. The dead body is symbolic. It can be an unsupportive person. It can be a bad habit, such as smoking, drug use, drinking, or lack of physical activity. It can also be a fear that prevents you from moving forward.

Again, self examination or working with a professional, such as a physician, counselor, or therapist, will reveal the dead bodies and possible solutions for removing them.

Panic Attack at 35,000 Feet

A dead body almost stopped me from achieving my goal of running a marathon on all seven continents. In July, 2004, I  headed to Europe. It was my first long plane trip. The plane wasn't full and I was able to occupy two seats. I combined the multi-country business trip with a side visit to Denmark for the marathon. Everything went smoothly.

A year later, I prepared to visit Australia to run a marathon on my birthday. Since I had to switch airline carriers, I had no control over the seating arrangements. Furthermore, the plane was packed with about 200 middle and high school students heading to Sydney for a music retreat.

I was assigned "the seat from hell," a window seat. I prefer isle seats due to my leg length. I can put one or both legs in the isle to stretch out. Now, I was shoved in a tight corner with no way to easily get out. When the person in front of me reclined their seat, it was about a foot from my face. I felt like I was in a sardine can. Minutes later, I felt a small panic attack approaching. As it turned out, tight spaces were my "dead body."

I left my seat and found a flight attendant. I pulled out my credit cards and asked to be moved to business class. It didn't matter how much it cost. Unfortunately, business class was full and he couldn't conduct the transaction anyway.

I explained my problem and he offered some helpful tips to make the flight bearable. If I hadn't acknowledged and cut this dead body lose, I would not have flown to China, Antarctica, Argentina, and Kenya to complete my goal.

The dead body can also be a person, such as a relative, spouse, close friend, or co-worker. It's the person who offers you discouragement, however small. They may even discourage you "for your own good."

Since they don't want to see you fail, they'll discourage you taking a risk, moving outside of your comfort zone (or the comfort zone they've built for you), and exploring something new.

Unfortunately, some dead bodies are close family members. They'll try to use the relationship to satisfy their personal needs at your expense. After all, they're family. And family members don't turn  their backs on each other. They're supposed to support each other, regardless of the circumstances. This is a "guilt trip." Your hard earned money was their money. And their money was their money.

A morning talk show host described this situation as "spider love." If you ask a spider, "Who do you love?" Their response is, "The fly." He catches the fly in his web and wraps it up in the web. When he's hungry, he sucks the juice out of the fly. The spider truly loves the fly. He sucks the life right out of it.

You have to recognize the spiders and dead bodies in your life and determine how to deal with them before you can successfully execute your plan. I realized that people wanted me to sacrifice my dreams and hard earned accomplishments for their irresponsible behavior and small comfort zones. I made a conscious decision to keep those close relatives and other individuals at a distance.

I had to cut the rope, drop the dead bodies, and kill the spiders for my personal sanity and success.

"You cannot fix, what you cannot face."

- James Baldwin

Running to Leadership

Managing Unplanned Events & Stress

When a crisis arises, such as an unplanned event, immediately classify it into one of three categories:

1. Observe – This is an event that you have absolutely no control over. Therefore, don't stress out over it. You must accept it and plan for it.
2. Influence – If you can influence the outcome of an event to your advantage, then try to do that. Keep in mind that someone else has control over the event. Thus, you should not be stressed over their decision. It's their right to control the outcome.
3. Control – This is an event that you can control. Since you have control, you shouldn't stress out over your decision. You decide what's in your best interest and take the appropriate action.

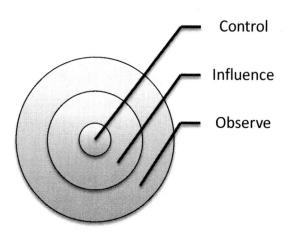

Running to Leadership

Another way to look at these three areas is to compare them with children. You can control a baby. When the child starts school, you can influence their behavior. When they graduate from high school, you can only observe them!!!

Fin Del Mundo Marathon White Out

On the eve of Argentina's Fin Del Mundo Marathon, we were looking down at the beautiful city of Ushuaia. In less than a minute, the snow was falling so fast, that the visibility was reduced to less than 50 yards.

About 15 minutes later, the snow stopped. Throughout the day we saw the weather change from perfect running temperatures to blinding snowstorms in a matter of minutes.

We couldn't control or influence the weather. The only thing that we could control was the clothing we wore. Thus, we didn't worry about the weather. Instead, we focused on our clothes.

Running to Leadership

We finally decided to dress in layers. Instead of wearing a single layer of heavy, winter clothes, we would wear multiple layers of light shirts, pants, and jackets. If the weather warmed up, we could easily remove the outer layers of clothes, tie them around our waist, and remain cool. This pre-planning allowed us to finish the marathon with minimal stress.

Procrastination

Procrastination is a major problem for me. It's my drug and I'm a recovering addict. Once an addict always an addict. It's easy to slip back into this problem if you aren't aware of your actions—or should I say, lack of actions.

Thus, I constantly fight not to procrastinate. I realized that by developing a good project plan, task list, or to do list, I decrease the probability of procrastination. I hold myself accountable for making the deadline. I try to:

- Break up the work into small chucks.
- Commit to a specific start date. This should not be January 1st. Too many people start life changing events on this same stress-filled date. If something is important enough to begin on January 1st, then it's important enough to begin today.
- Identify a specific end date. If the task doesn't have an end date, it doesn't have to be finished!!!
- Think about the final celebration and reward.
- Consider the number of people that you'll let down, such as your resources, if you're late.

Also, I take advantage of PC-based tools, such as MS Outlook, to set up reminders and alerts about upcoming events and tasks.

Delegating

Nobody can do it better than you can. You know how to do it your way. You can do it the right way. You do it yourself.

I was responsible for a highly visible major software implementation project. If we failed, we expected to hear about it in the U.S. Congress and read about it in the news media. Failure may have led to the agency's closure.

I worked with my project team to develop a detailed project plan. After we identified the tasks, dependencies, durations, and dates, we assigned resources to the tasks. Due to its importance, I was involved in many tasks. The plan was complete.

Later that day, I discovered a new report in the project planning software. It was a "resource leveling" report. It indicated that I was way overcommitted on the project. Based on my assigned tasks, I needed to work several hundred hours a week or learn to trust my staff and to delegate. I decided to delegate.

Watch Your Step – Leaf, Rock, Ankle

A friend went for a run on a beautiful fall day. He saw a leaf on the ground and decided to step on it. This simple act ended his running season, because beneath the leaf was a rock. As his foot landed on the leaf, the rock threw him off balance. He fell and broke his ankle, and his running season was over.

At one company, there was a business executive, who insisted on being the BMOC (big man on campus). He was a boastful "Type A" personality. He had to be better than everyone at everything.

His Director of Finance decided to become a runner. She slowly worked her way up to running three miles a day. He too decided to take up the sport and worked his way up to four miles a day. Afterwards, he quickly began boasting about his running accomplishments and became "the go-to guy" about all things related to running.

The BMOC hired an employee, who was both an experienced marathoner and bicyclist. For the executive, the marathon was too challenging. So, he took up bicycling. After several months of trying to keep up with the new employee, he blew out his knee. He lost his divisional "athletic" title to the unassuming new employee.

This executive decided to get rid of his athletic competitor. However, there wasn't anything to support the termination. In fact, the executive resorted to fabricating his supporting documentation. The terminated employee filed charges of wrongful termination and proceeded to seek legal remedies.

The executive was shocked. Later, he confided in a co-worker: "I thought he was like a little poodle. I didn't realize that he was really a pit bull." When the smoke cleared, the executive was asked to leave the company.

In both situations, people underestimated the impact of a seemingly harmless entity: a leaf and a seemingly passive individual. Leaves blow in the wind and easily crumble in our hands. The executive felt the same way about the individual. Just as the runner broke his ankle, the executive broke his career. You must focus on items beneath the surface and not become over-confident.

Running to Leadership

When in Doubt ... Stop

At six feet tall, I weighed over 190 pounds and had less than 10% body fat. I was built more like a pro football running-back than a distance runner. This meant that it would be difficult for me to win trophies or to meet the qualifying standard for the Boston Marathon.

 I'd have to lose weight to lower my marathon times. However, instead of losing fat to become lighter and faster, I'd have to lose muscle. Since I liked my muscular physique, I gave up my dreams of losing weight, getting faster, and placing in marathons.

Fortunately, race directors became "sensitive" to the plight of non-traditional marathoners. They began offering weight divisions. These usually started at around 140 and 190 pounds for women and men, respectively.

For this reason, the Dallas Trails Marathon was my favorite race. It was my first marathon that had weight divisions. Also, the entire course was at my favorite training spot, Dallas' White Rock Lake. I had run thousands of miles there for my training.

Since it had between 150 and 200 finishers, I had an opportunity to place in my weight division. For five consecutive years, I had placed in the 205 to 219 pound weight division. One year, the race directors decided to make things interesting. They wrote our weight on our legs. Thus, you definitely knew who was in your division. Needless to say, your objective during the race was to not let anyone in your division pass you.

After the gun sounded, the runners quickly settled into their race pace. This was one of the advantages of smaller marathons. Most marathoners are veterans and don't start out to fast. We don't need pace groups, bands along the course, or lots of fanfare. All we need is a well marked course, aid stations, and traffic control at the intersections.

After the first mile, I noticed a runner was just behind me, over my shoulder. He was still there after the second and third miles. He looked to be in my weight division. I looked over my shoulder and made a friendly suggestion for him to join me. Since we're going the same pace, he may as well pull even with me and we could talk and run together. He merely grunted and stayed behind. I could hear his breathing and his footsteps.

At this point, I realized that he was drafting off of me. Drafting allows an individual to save energy by remaining in the leader's slipstream. The leader expends more energy, while the follower may save 5% to 10% of their energy.

Migratory birds use this technique when they fly in the "V" formation, and race car drivers use this technique to save fuel. As the individuals approach the finish line, the follower usually has enough energy to pull even with leader and pass them in the final stretch. I believed this was what my "following friend" had in mind. I'd lead for 26 miles and he'd pass in the last 365 yards.

My objective was simple: to shake my friend loose. I tried everything in the book. As the leader, you control the pace and you (and only you) know when you're going to change the pace. I would suddenly surge or slow down. Since I carried my own fluids, I ran through the water stops. I'd speed up on the turns and up hills. I slowed down in the sun to bake him.

After sixteen miles, he was still there. I had heard his breathing and footsteps for what seemed like hours. Nothing I tried seemed to work. Around the 20-mile mark, I spotted my wife. She was standing alone in the middle of a field along the course. She had seen me several times along the race course and we had exchanged water bottles. And of course, she couldn't help but notice my "shadow."

I realized that I didn't have anything to lose and it was time for a new strategy, so I came to a complete stop and talked with my wife. My shadow didn't have any reason to stop. He reluctantly ran on ahead.

She said, "You must be upset. That guy must have gotten on your last nerve for you to just stop." After drinking some fluids, I remarked, "It's easy to follow and be the hunter. Now it's time for him to see how it is to be the leader and be hunted."

This was a very risky move on my part. I let him get about 200 yards ahead. However, we still had 6.2 miles to go and he was on my home turf. I made two major decisions. First, I would focus on maintaining a steady pace. Second, if I caught my shadow, I would "blow by him" so fast and look so strong doing it that he'd be so demoralized he would not try to catch up with me.

At around twenty-three miles, I spied my prey. He was taking walking breaks. My unpredictable surges and slowdowns had evidently reduced him to walking. A hundred yards before I reached him, I mentally gathered myself together, focused on my breathing, and ran with a very fluid stride. At twenty-five yards, I blew by him and kept on striding. He didn't even attempt to keep up. He was completely spent and never caught me.

An international company hired me to oversee a major IT project to implement a complex, new business software and technology. This replaced their existing accounts payable, accounts receivable, procurement, general ledger, fixed assets, and other applications. I was considered an expert in this area with over ten years of hands-on project management experience.

The project had started a couple months before my arrival. Since the company didn't have any prior experience with these applications and technology, they had hired a consulting firm. Their job was to create a project plan and implement the applications. I believed the company hired me because they were unsure about the quality and output from the consulting firm.

Upon arriving, I met with my staff. A meeting with the consultants quickly followed. During this meeting, I asked for a copy of the project schedule. They said, "No problem." An hour later, the junior partner (JP) delivered the document. It contained all of the parts of a good schedule, including the following:

√ Task name
√ Start date
√ End date
√ Duration
√ Resources
√ Percentage complete
√ Comments
√ Task's relationships to other tasks
√ Critical path
√ Comments

Just as I was getting excited about this wonderful schedule, it suddenly ended after two weeks. There was an estimated eight or nine months before the project would be completed. My first thought was that the printer must have run out of paper, and perhaps the partner had gone to refill it and would return with the rest of schedule. So, I just continued working on other tasks.

A few days later, he had still not returned with the rest of the document. I inquired about the project schedule and he returned with an updated version. Again, I dove into the schedule, only to see that it stopped after two weeks.

I immediately called the JP back in my office and asked for the rest of the schedule. He explained that they'd only allow me to see two weeks into the schedule. They felt that their project schedule was proprietary. Furthermore, if I had the entire schedule, I could implement the project with them.

I explained that it's impossible to run a nine-month project with only a two-week schedule at a time. How would people know when they could take vacation? You can't get cheap flights and book hotels two weeks out; you need at least a month. I said, "This project is costing us over a million dollars and you won't show me a complete schedule?"

I offered to sign a non-disclosure agreement, but they still refused. This wasn't rocket science. It might be daunting to a novice, but after ten years of experience, it should be a snap. However, the JP and his fellow partners refused to budge. They believed they were so far along in the project and so imbedded in our organization that they were not replaceable. Who in their right mind would stop the project? A marathoner.

That Friday, I reviewed the consulting firm's contract, and then I called in another consulting firm and explained the situation. I told them if they provided me with a complete project schedule, the contract was theirs. They delivered the schedule on Monday morning.

After reviewing the schedule in detail, I called in the JP's firm and explained that since I could only see the schedule planned two weeks into the future, I could only see them working on the project for another two weeks. They were handed their two-week notice per the terms of the contract.

Again, no matter how much pressure you're under, take a few moments to stop and think.

Relaxing and Uphill Battles

I participated in biathlons for cross training. This consisted of biking and running various events. The Mesquite "Beat the Heat" Biathlon was my favorite. It was one of the few biathlons that had the bike leg first, followed by the run.

They allowed drafting during the bike leg, since it could not be controlled during the mass start. As it turned out, cycling was actually my strongest sport, although I didn't pursue it for various reasons.

First, it was more expensive than running. I was the sole supporter for my family, and we were "economically challenged." It would have been very difficult (and selfish of me) to justify an expensive bike over a mortgage, food, and school clothes.

Second, it was time consuming. The time needed to perform the weekly maintenance on a bicycle could be spent with my family instead. Running shoes required considerably less maintenance.

Lastly, running was much more portable and weather tolerant. It was easier (and cheaper) to pack my running gear for a lengthy out-of-town trip than to pack a bike, and it was easier to run in the rain and snow than it was to cycle in the same conditions. It was also very  time consuming to clean a bike after a ride in the rain.

During the bike leg of the biathlon, I managed to stay with the lead group of about five cyclists. Thus, the race was going to be determined by who was the fastest runner. I felt that, based on my marathon background and endurance, I should place well in the race – if not win it.

Because of my previous experiences at this race, I was familiar with the course. The running route used an "out and back" layout. We ran out to a point, turned around and ran back.

Running to Leadership

This type of course can be mentally challenging for the race's leader. The runners behind you are watching for any sign of change in your running style, because this may indicate weakness.

Is your head suddenly bobbing more from side to side? Do your shoulders look tight? Is your stride getting shorter? Do you look uncomfortable?

The real challenge comes when you reach the turnaround point. Now you must face the person who's been watching and studying your every move from behind. They're looking for a kink in your armor: your weakness. If they see it or sense it, they go in for the kill. This is also what we face as business executives.

During the first leg of the run, I focused on maintaining a fast pace. I could hear a runner's foot steps behind me. He wasn't going to let me get away. My face was contorted in pain as I tried to fight him off and my pain. I dared not look around, because this would have been a major sign of weakness.

As I approached the bright orange turnaround cone, I realized that this was an opportunity to plant a seed of doubt in his mind. I relaxed my face, caught my breath, and made the U-turn.

As we approached one another, I said, in my most relaxed voice, "Man, it's getting hot out here." I wanted him to begin thinking about the heat.

Running to Leadership

About half of a mile from the finish line, we had to climb a nasty hill. However, once we reached the top, the finish line was only about one hundred yards down hill.

As I drew nearer to the base of the hill, the other runner's footsteps were still pounding in my ears. I was physically exhausted. However, I wasn't going to give up the fight.

My strategy was to appear completely relaxed while going up the hill, regardless of the amount of pain I was feeling. One hundred percent of my focus was on looking good, smooth, and in control. I reached the top of the hill with the runner still behind me. Momentum carried me across the finish line. The other runner finished a few seconds behind me.

As we congratulated one another, he said, "You looked so smooth going up the hill that I stopped trying to catch you. I thought you were holding back and still had something in your tank, so I focused on maintaining my position and not getting passed."

 As a business leader, it's important to maintain a level-head under pressure. If your staff members see you explode, they may decide to withhold valuable negative information from you out of fear that you'll go after them. Thus, they may notify you of bad news later rather than sooner.

Running to Leadership

One of my previous employers implemented an annual management-evaluation system. The staff evaluated their immediate manager and their overall divisional management style. The employee evaluations of management were just as important (and carried just as much weight) as their manager's evaluation of them. The manager evaluations were anonymous, and written comments were transcribed and included with the quantitative evaluation results.

Our manager received one of the worse ratings. It was so bad that the human resources (HR) executive arranged a meeting with him and his employees. The objective was for our manager to respond to our concerns. He was to learn from his mistakes and then take the appropriate corrective actions.

The HR executive laid out the ground rules: this was to be a meeting with free, open, and honest discussions about the evaluation results; and there would be no retaliation against any of the team members. There was only one problem. The team knew that our manager was vindictive.

The room was quiet; you could hear a pin drop. After a few minutes, the HR executive repeated the ground rules and reiterated that there would be absolutely no retaliation. The room remained silent.

A few more minutes passed as we looked around the room. Finally, our manager began yelling and pounding his fist on the table. Almost on cue, without saying a word, the entire team looked at the HR VP. The meeting was ended. Within a month, the manager was demoted and then, later, he was terminated.

The manager was ineffective because he was unap-proachable. He exploded at the slightest sign of a stressful situation. Since nobody wanted to face his wrath, they withheld bad news until the very last second, by which time it was usually too late to effec-tively deal with the problem.

During my performance evaluation, he downgraded me and commented, "You don't get excited when problems occurred."

I asked, "Did the problems get resolved correctly in a timely manner?"
"Yes."
"So, what's the real problem?"
He said, "You just don't look concerned. You don't yell or appear mad or angry. That running stuff you do must make you unemotional."

After a long pause, I finally responded. "The time spent losing control and yelling and screaming could be spent thinking about solutions and implementing them. However, to make you happy, next time I'll allo-cate five minutes for screaming before solving the problem."

He was partly right about the running. It gave me the ability to think clearly and function well, while under pressure.

Killer Rocks

Killer rocks to marathoners aren't like the rock-monsters in sci-fi movies. They're the little rocks that get caught in our shoes. You may be able to run a couple of miles with a small rock rubbing against your foot; however, at some point you will have to stop and remove it. If you don't, it may cause a blister. If this goes untreated, it could lead to an infection, and if the infection isn't treated, it could even lead to amputation or death.

As a manager, we must constantly look for the little rocks and quickly take care of them. If not, the resulting infection may kill the project. Project managers typically schedule weekly status meetings in the same conference room. Similar meetings may be scheduled over several months.

At one company, I attended the initial status meeting for a project. Several people mentioned the lack of lighting in the room. The next week, their comments were repeated. This was a small rock in the project's shoe. I realized that without additional lighting, people may begin to view the project in a negative light. They may decide to skip the meetings or feel depressed as they entered the room. This wasn't the type of attitude I wanted for the team members. The room was a de-motivator.

Just as removing a rock from a shoe is easy, killing this potential rock monster was also easy. We circumvented the corporate red tape by purchasing desk lamps and a couple of tall lamps for the conference room. The team's attitude changed, and the project was ultimately a success.

Thinking Outside the Sox

David and I left work to run the nine-mile loop at Dallas' White Rock Lake. This was always a great relief after being cooped up in the office all day, and it was about a pleasant fifty degrees. We parked in our usual parking lot, changed into our shorts and singlets, and proceeded to run.

Unbeknownst to us, a very fast-moving cold front was moving into the area. Temperatures were expected to drop more than twenty-five degrees – to below freezing – in less than an hour. This was the perfect scenario for a disaster.

It felt great working up a sweat, as the miles clicked away. The wind was on our backs as we ran. Our bodies were heating up as the temperature was dropping, so we didn't notice the drop in degrees. In fact, we were excited to be moving that fast with a tailwind. After about four miles with the tailwind, we turned a corner. For the first time, we realized the wind's strength and the cold temperature. A few minutes later, we turned directly into the now-freezing winds. By that time, it was dark.

We realized that turning around wasn't a solution. Whichever way we ran, we still had 4.5 miles to go in-

Running to Leadership

to the wind, and we were acutely aware that there was almost nothing in the way of buildings to block the wind, and our sweat-soaked clothes were giving us the chills.

Cars were rarely seen in this area of the lake after dark, so catching a lift back to our cars was highly unlikely. Besides, who would stop their car on a dark road and let two strange, sweaty men sit on their car's upholstery? Jason or Freddy?

David and I were freezing. We knew that if we stopped to walk, it might be over for us, so we kept moving and talking. We discussed why neither of us had any children yet despite both being married. Our "extremities" were getting very cold against the wet, freezing cloth. (This was before high-tech, sweat-whisking, stay-dry fabric was developed.)

As we continued running, we talked about ways to keep our private parts warm. We couldn't run with our hands down our shorts; and besides, our hands were cold. We didn't have caps to shove down there either. We talked about removing our shirts, but they were also soaked and freezing. As we ran, we looked for anything, even newspaper and leaves, to shove down our shorts.

Then we realized that we had one piece of dry clothing that might do the trick ...our socks. So we stopped in the freezing winds, removed our socks, and very carefully put them in place. Not only did we finish the run, but later we each had two children.

Running to Leadership

In the heat (or coldness) of the situation, we focused on what was most important to us and prioritized accordingly. We looked for alternatives and used our limited resources to address a very critical problem. We had to think "outside of the sox."

Years later, I was divisional CIO with global responsibilities and staff in both the US and Europe. My project coordinator, James, walked in my office one day. He was a former military officer and one of the best project managers I had worked with. I had learned, that when he started a sentence with the word "sir," I needed to pay special attention to what was to follow.

He explained that our software-upgrade project might be in trouble. For several months, the project team had been looking for a contract programmer to write the data-conversion tie-out programs. These programs compared the financial data in the new and old systems. Any discrepancies had to be highlighted for future investigation.

These programs went beyond comparing the number of records in the old and new files; they also totaled key fields *and* compared the actual data in the two records. For example, 2+2 or 1+3 both equal 4; therefore, it wasn't enough to tally the fields. We had to compare each record as well.

The contractor had to understand financial accounting, programming, data-base structures, and the business software. This was an estimated six-week task, but after several months of looking nationwide, we had come up empty-handed.

James explained that the team was getting distracted by this now critical and as-yet unfilled position. He recalled that my background included all of these elements and asked whether I'd consider writing the programs.

I was speechless. It had been decades since I had done any kind of serious programming, and I didn't have six weeks to devote to writing programs. It could take me six weeks just to get back up to speed! However, the project was about to fail. Not wanting to say, "No" and, being politically correct, I told him I'd think about it.

During my evening run, I thought about the possible logic for the programs. I mentally wrote the first program and put it "on the shelf." Next, I wrote another program and set it aside. As I began thinking about the third program, I discovered a logical pattern to writing the programs.

The next morning, I asked our database administrator a few questions and got a special security clearance. He was surprised by my technical questions and curious about my motives. (He was unaware that I had taught collegiate database-design classes.)

I went back to my office and closed the door. In a few hours, I had generated over 120 of the 125 conversion tie-out programs. They all worked perfectly the first time.

Later that afternoon, we had a meeting to demonstrate the programs. People were stunned. Their "distraction" or excuse for failure was gone. Another programmer quickly wrote the remaining five programs the next day.

I had to think out of the box and discover new ways to work with old tools. Instead of just writing the programs, I had used a combination of pure logic, the programming language, database knowledge, and PC-based word processing and spreadsheet software applications to automatically produce the programs.

The Achievement Equation's Success Formula

The Achievement Equation's (AE) components are

I_G – Idea (Goals)
I_M - Incentive (Motivation)
I_P – Instructions (Plans)
I_E - Implementation (Execution)

Without a SMART idea (goal), you can't develop and follow instructions (a plan). An unclear goal yields an equally unclear result. A goal setter without both motivation and a plan is like a dreamer who stays in bed. Motivation is the string that connects the SMART goal, the plan, and the execution. Without motivation, the plan may never be developed or executed.

A highly motivated person without a plan is like a dog chasing his tail. There's just a lot of dust from where the dog was running. Action doesn't always yield results.

Let's assume that each component is represented by a binary value. That's to say, each component's value is either zero or one. The Individual Achievement Equation becomes

$$I_A = I_G \times I_M \times I_P \times I_E$$

This is a multiplicative equation. Any number multiplied by zero yields zero. In our equation,

- You either set a <u>SMART goal</u> (value = 1) or don't (value = 0).
- You're either <u>highly motivated</u> to reach your SMART goal (value = 1) or not (value = 0).
- You're either highly motivated to develop <u>a good plan</u> to reach your SMART goal (value = 1) or you try to wing it (value = 0).
- You're either highly motivated <u>to execute</u> the plan to reach your SMART goal (value = 1) or you do nothing (value = 0).

Since the equation is
$$I_A = I_G \times I_M \times I_P \times I_E = (\text{Zero or One})$$

Achievement always equals one or zero. Thus, if you fail to follow through on any one of the components, AE equals zero. In other words, you achieve nothing.

Running to Leadership

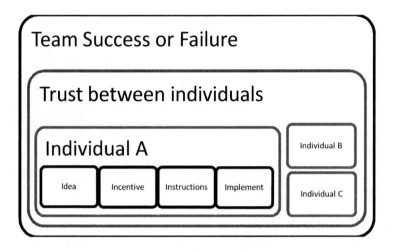

When a team of individuals is involved, the team's success and effectiveness is based on the trust that the individuals have between one another.

$$T_A = I_{A1} \times I_{A2} \times I_{A3} \times I_{A+} \times Trust$$

The more the team members trust one another, the higher the trust value, the faster the team works together, and the project costs less. The less the team members trust one another, the lower the trust value, the slower the team works together, and the more expensive the project becomes.

All of us know successful people who achieved goals without fully implementing all of these components. They had luck. The equation may be modified to allow for luck (assigned value = L). Luck is also binary.

The equation now becomes

$$I_A = (I_G \times I_M \times I_P \times I_E) + L$$

Now, any or all of the values for G, M, P, and E may be zero. If luck is available (value = 1), then the goal is achieved. The problem with luck, such as winning the lottery, is that you can't control it or predict when it will occur.

What's Next?

For as long as I've been setting and achieving goals, people tend to ask me one question, "What's next?" Whether I'm travelling internationally or taking a training run around Dallas' White Rock Lake, most conversations lead to same question, "What's next?"

Over the years, I began to notice four interesting reactions or by-products to achieving goals.

First, people live vicariously through the accomplishments of achievers. They want to say that they personally know someone who has achieved an individual goal. It could be completing a triathlon, bicycling across the U.S., competing in an open water swimming competition, or earning an undergraduate degree in your forties. You become the person that your friends will talk about at happy hours, the water cooler, and at church. You made it!!!

Running to Leadership

Second, people expect you to continue to set and achieve goals. They don't expect failure. They expect you to succeed. They'll want to be able to continue telling their friends about your adventures and accomplishments. They become your cheerleaders and supporters. Everyone wants to support a winner. And you're a winner that they can bank on.

During the Great Wall of China Marathon tour, several of the runners bonded together. One evening at dinner, we began discussing what we would do after we finished marathons on all seven continents.

For the first time, I began to realize that life without a goal was dull and unexciting. It was actually depressing to think about life after running marathons on the seven continents. Since I was the computer geek and brought my laptop on the trip, I was given the task of finding the Seven Wonders of the World on the Internet. Yes, we were contemplating running marathons in or near the locations of the Wonders.

Much to our surprise, there were many different "seven wonders" to choose from:

- Ancient Wonders
- Modern Wonders
- Underwater Wonders
- Architectural Wonders
- Man-Made Wonders

Running to Leadership

We even talked about running marathons on the seven continents again, but running them on islands. This might take us to:

- Jamaica (North America)
- New Zealand (Oceania)
- Japan (Asia)
- King George Island (Antarctica)
- Madagascar (Africa)
- Galapagos Islands (South America)
- Iceland (Europe)

We realized that no matter what goal we set our eyes on, it would be exciting and fun.

The third thing about achieving goals relates to heroes. During a training run, I was joined by a stranger. He looked to be in his sixties. As it turned out, he was from my hometown of St. Louis. Instinctively, I asked him about the baseball Cardinals season.

He told me that he used to follow baseball religiously. Several years ago, he suffered a heart attack and had a triple bypass. While he was recovering, he decided to change his lifestyle.

He got his doctor's approval and began running. Now, whenever he wants to see an athlete, he just looks in the mirror. He became his own hero.

Running to Leadership

After our conversation, I began noticing something about distance runners. Instead of wearing the jerseys of professional athletes, we wear our race t-shirts. Perhaps it's our way of saying that we're our own heroes and athletes. As you set and achieve goals, don't be surprised if you become less interested in the lives of entertainers and athletes and more focused on your own goals.

The last observation about achievers is that they become the best cheerleaders. They've "been through the fire" and "crossed the burning sands." They know what it's like to have to dig deep when you feel that no one else is around to help you. For these reasons, achievers tend to motivate and inspire others in reaching their goals. In turn, these people may help you in your future endeavors or adventures.

Running to Leadership

GOMOPLEX^{TM} is a life-style supplement. It's taken men-tally. After years of research, it was determined that by combining four previously separate elements into one supplement, a synergic effect occurs. People have been known to achieve their personal and professional goals. GOMOPLEX^{TM} is based on the Achievement Equation.

POSSIBLE SIDE EFFECTS OF GOMOPLEX^{TM} include a sense of accomplishment, personal and professional fulfillment, excitement, happiness, priceless moments, and high levels self confidence. These side effects are contagious and may spread to friends and relatives. GOMOPLEX^{TM} users have been known to break sales records, complete projects on time, within budget, and to specifications, improve productivity, graduate from school, run marathons around the world, and finish triathlons.

WARNINGS: GOMOPLEX^{TM} should not be taken by people who want to lead dull and directionless lives. It should not be taken by people who want to be lazy or inactive. People, who don't want to achieve goals, should not take GOMOPLEX^{TM}. They may find that they'll exceed their personal expectations, overcome their fears, and accomplish something spectacular.

GOMOPLEX^{TM} has been approved by the FDA (Fun and Daring Administration).

International Marathon Race Day Diaries

This section contains the pages from my race day journals. The complete journals are in my book, <u>Running Shoes are Cheaper Than Insulin: Marathon Adventures on All Seven Continents</u>.

Running Shoes Are Cheaper Than Insulin:

Marathon Adventures On All Seven Continents

(Yes. That's a cheetah on the course.)

By
Anthony "Tony" Reed, CPA

Running to Leadership

Tailwinds Marathon – Copenhagen, Denmark

Date: July 25, 2004
Marathon Number: 58
International Marathon Number: 2
Inspirational Song: "We're A Winner" performed by The Impressions (with Curtis Mayfield)

Running to Leadership

According to the website, "The Tailwind marathon is arranged by runners for runners as a back-to-basic marathon race without grand prizes etc.—which is reflected in the start fee, which is 150 Danish kroner (DKK), 20 US dollars or 25 euro." The race was so low key that there would not be any:

- Printed material - Everything would be handled via the website.
- Race numbers.
- Manned aid stations – You brought your own electrolytes.
- Medical aid stations or assistance.
- Finisher medals.
- Portable toilets – You had to use the toilets in the train depots. This assumes that you know their location along the course.
- Closed off streets – The traffic would be moving at its regular pace.
- Street crossing guards – You had to watch out for cars and obey the traffic signals.
- Sag wagon – The directions for quitting were also posted on the website. "If you drop out of the race, you can take the "Kystbanetog" (train) towards Elsinore Station (every 20th minute) or bus 388 from "Strandvejen" to the finishing line. We recommend that you carry a yellow card (non-used ticket for multiple destinations) during the race. The yellow card can be bought at train stations or in buses within 30 kilometres from Copenhagen. Please inform the staff at the nearest depot if you're dropping out."

Running to Leadership

The website summed up the demands on the partici-
pants by stating, "Basically, participation is on your
own responsibility—Pay attention to your body and
the surrounding world." Needless to say, this wasn't
anything like the mega-marathons in the US.

Since there was a time limit for finishing the marathon, we had to submit our fastest times for either the
half marathon or the full marathon in the previous
twelve months for review. The results were subsequently posted on the race's website.

Much to my surprise, I would finish dead last by about
30 minutes!!! I estimated that after the first twenty minutes of the race, I would lose sight of the runners
and be on my own. I was also the only American out
of the 58 runners.

Therefore, for the first time in my life, I had to prepare
to finish in last place in a marathon without any assistance in a foreign country where I didn't speak the
language. This was going to be an adventure.

Race Day Activities

The morning was prefect as I left the hotel around
7AM. It was overcast and cool. The bus and train
rides went very well. I took care of my personal business in the depot's restroom and walked to the starting line. Much to my surprise, there was only one other person at the starting line 45 minutes before the
start. People finally started arriving about 15 minutes
later.

Running to Leadership

Boxes were set out for us to put in our bottles of water or electrolytes. The boxes were labeled in 5K increments from 5K through 35K. Since there were no manned aid stations, you placed your fluids in the appropriate box and they were dropped off on tables along the route. I placed my clearly identifiable bottles in the 15K (9.3-mile) and 30K (18.6-mile) boxes.

Fortunately, as luck would have it, the race director had enough paid entrants to afford race numbers.
As soon as the race started, so did the rain. It continued to rain throughout the day. After 3K, I was running alone. After 5K, I didn't see the runners in front of me. Fortunately, we had kilometer signs along the course. Thus, the only way I could tell if I was still on the course was by seeing a kilometer marking every 6 to 7 minutes.

I saw only one directional sign during the entire 26.2 miles. This wasn't bad until I approached a major intersection between 11K and 12K. I spotted a directional arrow that was nailed to a lamppost. Unfortunately, it was on one nail and was spinning around like a windmill.

I didn't even know if it was related to the race or another event. Since it was a point-to-point course, I knew that I wasn't supposed to turn around. Thus, I had a one in three chance of going in the right direction.

Running to Leadership

As luck would have it, I took the wrong turn. I made a right turn because I knew that the course followed the shoreline, which was on my right. Fortunately, since the race director was able to afford race numbers, a couple of motorists told me that I was off the course. Unfortunately, they didn't tell me which way to go when I returned to the "spinning arrow" intersection.

By this time, I had a 50-50 chance of picking the right direction. As luck would have it, I went the wrong way, again.

While I wasted over 20 minutes during this fiasco, I considered myself to be an explorer or adventurer. I told myself that if I could survive this low-key, no frills "runners" marathon in a foreign country in the wind and rain and communicate without knowing the language, then I could survive anything.

I was conservative regarding my fluid consumption. Since there weren't any easily accessible restrooms along the course, I wanted to avoid any pit stops. As I approached the 15K "aid table," I was relieved to see my water bottle. I decided to withhold some fluids in reserve.

At the 30K table, things went wrong. Someone had removed half of the electrolytes. I didn't know whether or not they drank from the bottle or just poured some out. I played it safe and left the bottle. I nursed my 15K to the finish line.

Running to Leadership

As I approached the finish line, I noticed my backpack with my dry clothes sitting in a puddle on the ground. My clothes were soaked. However, as I crossed the finish line, the race director, much to my surprise, handed me a finisher's medal. My time was five hours, thirty-four minutes, and twenty-eight seconds. I finished.

I was cold, wet, and starving. I walked about a mile to the metro train station (and the nearest restroom). Unfortunately, the food stand was closed. Thus, I sat in wet clothes for the one-hour return trip to the hotel by the metro train and bus. I left for the race at 7AM and returned to my room 12 hours later. After a hot shower, that Dominos pizza never tasted so good. While I finished dead last in the race, I finished in the top 50 and was the first American!!! There's always a bright side to finishing a marathon—if you look closely!!!

The Great Wall Marathon – Huangyaguan, China

Date: May 20, 2006
Marathon Number: 77
International Marathon Number: 4
Inspirational Song: "Once In A Life Time" performed by The Talking Heads

Running to Leadership

Race Report: Saturday, May 20 5:00 PM Dallas/Sunday, May 21 6:00 AM Beijing

It's 6AM the day after the marathon. I've been up since 5:30 revamping the China trip web pages while listening to and watching 2004 George Clinton's concert. For those who don't know me, this is an indication that I'm in a very, very good mood. I changed the website to allow even faster loading of the photos.

These photos are in sequential order from the start of the day until the end. I tried to take photos that show the changes in the running trail and different views from the trail. I'd like to thank the runners and race helpers who took my photo during the race.

A Special Message to the Non-Runners

This was the absolute toughest marathon I've ever run. This was my 77th marathon or ultra-marathon. A number of other veteran runners concurred. To help put this in perspective, my worst marathon (26.2-miles) finishing time was 5 hours, 45 minutes. This occurred in a marathon where the temperatures exceeded 100 degrees. I've also run a 50K (31.1-mile) ultra-marathon in 7 hours. It took me 7.5 hours to finish The Great Wall Marathon (GWM)!!!

The race started "flat" and proceeded up a long, steep hill on asphalt. Next, we entered the Great Wall area. Here, we encountered over 3,500 steps. These were of various heights. At times, we were walking along ledges. Again, most of these areas were too steep to

145

run either up or down. However, the scenery was beautiful.

After departing the main section of the wall, we proceeded down a steep dirt trail. It was actually too steep for most of us to run down. Again, to help put this in perspective, it took me two hours to run the first six miles. This compares to one hour under normal circumstances.

Over 100 photos were taken during the race. This was the first time I've taken photos during a race. This gave me an excuse to stop and take a much-needed rest. (Years later, this will be my excuse for not running the race any faster.)

Throughout the marathon, there were a number of cynical and sarcastic signs along the road. They were usually strategically placed. I couldn't help but take these pictures. (I didn't have to ask the signs to stand still!!!)

On the bus at 3 AM

Running to Leadership

The runners were met by a band (in the flatbed truck) and dancers.

In the arena at the start of the marathon.

Running to Leadership

The start of the first major hill to get to the Great Wall.

The sign says it all.

Running to Leadership

A major hill & the entrance to the Great Wall

Running to Leadership

Me at the Great Wall and the sign that greeted us.

The start of running on the Great Wall.

A view from The Wall. This gives some perspective about
how far we had to go.

Running to Leadership

One of the first ledges. Note the drop off and no railing. OSHA would have issues with the contractor.

Running to Leadership

The steep stairs and another ledge. If you think this is difficult in the beginning, the marathoners had to re-peat this process AFTER running over 20 miles!!!

Running to Leadership

I'm smiling because my first pass of the wall is over. However, the steep dirt trail begins.

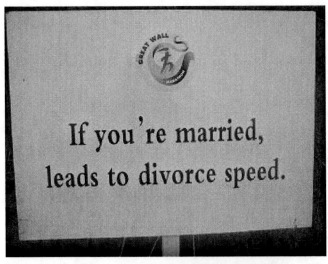

Some things get lost in translation. We never figured out the meaning of the sign. This kept us from thinking about our pain.

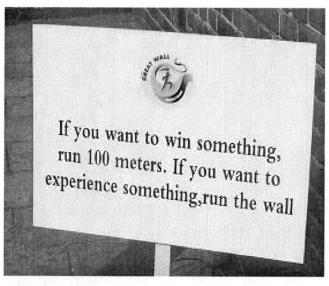

If you want to win something, run 100 meters. If you want to experience something, run the wall

Thank goodness we didn't have to run through the maze.

Running to Leadership

Beautiful scenery and a rocky farm road.

Running to Leadership

I was as much an "attraction" in the small villages as in Beijing. A non-English speaking runner motioned for me to join the group of children in this photo.

We passed numerous beehives along the way.

Running to Leadership

We had to run to the white tower in the background.
(Another hill!!!)

A race without hills is like
coffee without caffeine

We had too much caffeine during the race.

Running to Leadership

After running on asphalt, we switched back to a dirt road.

Scenes of me on the road and at 29K (17.98 miles). I'm smiling because posing gives me a chance (excuse) to rest.

Running to Leadership

Having successfully made my way back to the arena, I had to go back up the steep trail to get to the wall again. (By the way, the word "steep" is not overused in any of the descriptions!!!)

The bridge-like structure in the middle of this photo is the arena. You can't have a fear of heights and run this race.

From the same spot in the previous photo, this shows how much of the wall I still have to cover. Yes, I have to go to the second guard tower!!!

Running to Leadership

Excuse the puns from Michael Jackson. I'm "Off the Wall"
and I stopped because I got enough.

Running to Leadership

Back at the arena where I started seven hours, twenty-eight minutes, and forty-five seconds later.

The race ended with a well-deserved shower and massage.

Running to Leadership

Antarctica Marathon – King George Island

Date: February 26, 2007
Marathon Number: 82
International Marathon Number: 5
Inspirational Song:
"A Psychoalphadiscobetabioaquadoloop" performed by Parliament

Running to Leadership

Race Day Report: King George Island, Antarctica, February 26 (Marathon Day)

We were awakened at 6:15 to begin preparation for the marathon. Unlike most marathons, we had to be transported to the starting line by zodiacs. Unlike China's marathon, I was limited in the number of photos that I took. (That translates to a faster marathon finishing time.)

With temperatures at or below freezing and 40 mile/hour winds, my fingers froze when I removed my gloves. At one point, I thought that I had frost bite. Another time, I actually dropped the camera in a puddle of water because I couldn't feel it.

The Great Wall of China Marathon is the closet comparison to this marathon. The GWC had man-made obstacles (over 3,400 steps). This one had Mother Nature's obstacles—steep hills and glaciers and weather.

The zodiacs had to transport about 200 people from two ships. It took about 15 minutes per trip. We landed at the Russian Research Station called Bellinghausen.

Bellinghausen was an Antarctic explorer. Technically speaking, we were in Russia. Since the course took us through the Uruguay, China, and Chile research stations, we were also in those countries according to the treaties. Antarctica is the only continent without any countries.

Running to Leadership

You can see from the photos below that we had to bundle up in our waterproof clothes and boots just to be transported to the race site. Also, you'll notice the snowflakes. We had debated about what would be the best conditions; at or below freezing or above freezing.

While we may feel better with the temps above freezing, it would increase the amount of mud we may have to run through. On the other hand, temps below freezing may lead to frost bite.

Running to Leadership

Running to Leadership

The Russian buildings were situated on stilts. After we landed, we changed into our running gear under the buildings. We left our gear there for the duration of the race. About ten minutes after my zodiac landed, the race started.

The scenery was almost indescribable. It was like looking at a black-and-white photo. With the exception of the runners and man-made objects (i.e. buildings), everything was in shades of gray.

Prior to the trip, I tried running with a face mask. Unfortunately, it was difficult to breathe. So, I grew out my beard. For the first time, the hair on my face was longer than the hair on my head.

Running to Leadership

My face stayed warm, but my lips lost their feeling. When I drank, I couldn't feel the fluids. I didn't know if it went into my mouth or down my shirt. Also, the anti-fog solution stopped working on my sunglasses and I had to remove them. This created visibility problems since almost everything was white (and getting whiter with the snowfall) and very bright. I had nothing to protect my eyes from the UV rays.

In addition to being cold, Antarctica is very, very dry. After all, it never rains, only snows. Therefore, there's almost no moisture in the air. You have to keep telling yourself that although you're feeling hydrated and not sweating, you must continue to drink fluids.

Did I mention that the "aid stations" are really water bottles tossed in the snow? You find your bottle, take a drink, and put it back in the snow for your return trip. (All of the bottles were retrieved by the support staff after the race.)

Running to Leadership

The mud fields.

We left the starting line and headed towards the Uruguay Base. Along the way, we ran through ankle deep mud, crossed streams, and climbed many short, steep hills. However, absolutely nothing prepared us for Collins Glacier.

Running to Leadership

It's very difficult to take a photo that shows the challenges of Collins Glacier. The photo below shows the runners on the glacier at a distance.

To help put this in perspective, imagine yourself running on a treadmill at your local gym. After three miles of running, set the angle of the treadmill to 17 percent. (Most treadmills only go to 10 or 12 percent.)

Now, add an icy surface, snow blowing in your face, 40 MPH winds, and no shelter to hide from the wind. Oh, by the way, it's about a 3/4-mile from the glacier's bottom to the turnaround point. Unfortunately, this can't be simulated on a treadmill.

Your calves and thighs ache. Although gravity pulls you downhill, you have to brace for every step so you won't slip and fall. Thus, your thighs are screaming in pain.

Running to Leadership

Also, if you're running the marathon, you have to do this again around 17 miles!!! Here are a couple of views from the bottom and the turnaround point on the glacier. Unfortunately, none of these photos really illustrate the difficulty of this part of the course.

View from the bottom of the glacier.

View from the top of the glacier.

Running to Leadership

The glacier was a humbling experience. A number of marathoners decided to quit and just run the half marathon. I actually considered this. However, my thoughts turned to the 3,600 steps that we ran during the Great Wall of China Marathon.

I had to take it one step at a time. Evidently, I would make it to the top. (On my second trip up the glacier, I wore spikes.) I'll never complain about another hill again.

We retraced our steps back to Bellinghausen. The terrain was tough. We ran on lose rock, ice, snow, slush, and mud. Since many of us are also running the Fin Del Mundo Marathon, we were concerned about possible injuries.

Running to Leadership

We returned to Bellinghausen, ran through the Chilean Base, passed the Russian's Orthodox Church, and headed towards the Chinese "Great Wall" Base. We were told that after the Pope declared that Antarctica was Catholic, the Russians had their church constructed!!!

Along the way, we passed "Fur Seal Freeway." As luck would have it, we ran past seals and penguins. I also saw a fellow Texan from the Great Wall of China Marathon. Since we were on different ships, we hadn't seen each other since Argentina.

Fur seal on the marathon course.

Russian Orthodox Church.

Running to Leadership

After we reached the China base, we headed back to Bellinghausen. Half marathoners finished after one loop. However, full marathoners had to go through the loop a second time. This time, there were only a handful of people on the glacier.

So, you really had to concentrate and dig down deep, since there weren't other runners offering encouragement. This actually reminded me of the Great Wall of China Marathon. I had to concentrate on every single step to avoid falling.

This marathon was mentally and physically tough when you combine the weather conditions with the glacier climbs. I finished the marathon within about five minutes of my projected time. Considering the fact that I've been ill the past couple of days, that wasn't bad.

It's 10:30PM and I'm about to pass out. Goodnight.

Running to Leadership

Fin Del Mundo Marathon – Ushuaia, Argentina

Date: March 6, 2007
Marathon Number: 83
International Marathon Number: 6
Inspirational Song:
" A Psychoalphadiscobetabioaquadoloop" performed by Parliament

Running to Leadership

Race Day Report

The morning started with a 7:00AM bus ride to the start of the Fin Del Mundo Marathon. Most of us decided to dress in layers. Thus, we could peel off our clothes if the weather became warm. We were told during dinner that Fox TV would be taping the marathon and interviewing runners.

Naturally, I posed with the mascots of the race.

An interesting little side note, I was told that beavers, foxes, and rabbits were not native to this area. They were introduced to be hunted for their fur. However, since they didn't have any natural enemies, their population exploded. During our bus ride, we probably saw over 50 rabbits.

Running to Leadership

The following photos are scenes from the race course.

Running to Leadership

While parts of the race were very beautiful, the section that passed near the airport was extremely windy. I felt sorry for anyone under 125 pounds. The wind was going to blow them away. One runner remarked that he was handed a cup of water at an aid station. Before he could put it to his lips, the wind blew the water completely out of his cup.

A fellow runner and I dragged our way through about 15 to 20 miles of the marathon when his wife appeared. There's nothing like having your spouse meet you on the race course and drag you to the finish line. She had finished the race earlier.

The last few miles of the race were spent talking about food. All I wanted was either a Snickers bar or orange/tangerine Jelly Belly Beans. After we finished, we walked a couple of blocks to the taxi stand.

As luck would have it, the taxi stand was right in front of a grocery store. Yes, I ran/limped in and bought

Running to Leadership

five Snickers!!! I gave two to the husband and wife team, ate two on the spot, and saved one for a midnight snack. (I'll have it with my ham and cheese sandwich, which was smuggled from the bar.)

With this trip, I've completed my 82nd and 83rd marathons on my fifth and sixth continents. Africa is the only remaining continent in my quest. It's 11:30PM and I still have to pack for an 8AM departure. When I arrive in Dallas, I'll have a craving for IHOP pancakes (BIG HINT!!!!).

Goodnight!!!

Running to Leadership

Safaricom Marathon – Lewa Wildlife Sanctuary

Date: June 23, 2007
Marathon Number: 7
International Marathon Number: 7
Inspirational Song: "Chocolate City" performed by Parliament

Running to Leadership

Race Day Report

We were awakened at 4:30AM to prep for the race and grab a bite to eat. I ate the cup of noodles since it's easily digestible and contains carbs and salt. We loaded into the Land Rovers at 5:30 for the ride to the race.

It occurred to me that this is the first race where I won't be in the minority. The weather was cool and cloudy. Since there wasn't very much shade on the course, we hoped the sun stayed hidden.

Everywhere we looked, we saw children. People were running in every type of shoe imaginable. We saw a herd of zebras running across the road. Airplanes and helicopters buzzed overhead to keep the more dangerous animals away.

Running to Leadership

Yes...That's a special National Black Marathoners' Association running jersey made especially for the race. It will be retired to a shadow box with the trip's mementos.

This was not your typical Boston, Chicago, or NYC Marathon. After the race started, I didn't recall seeing any buildings. The largest crowd, not counting the aid station workers, was about 40 people during the first lap. It was about five people during the second lap. However, the landscape and scenery were beautiful. Plus, the bugs didn't bother me.

The weather was perfect. The sun stayed behind the clouds and kept the temperature cool. I didn't even have to wear my hat during the race. A slight breeze also helped. We followed our plan of drinking plenty of electrolytes (and orange jelly beans) during the race.

I ran most of the way with an Australian. We kept within sight of another runner. We used photo-taking, Vaseline-rubbing, and rocks-in-shoes opportunities to take breaks. The company was very well appreciated. (I think that we felt that four or six eyes looking out for animals was much better than two eyes.)

Running to Leadership

A warning sign that two hills are ahead.

Running to Leadership

After I crossed the finish line, I learned that one of my Texas tour mates won her age group. Since I carried cash in my "Batman utility belt," I decided to get Paul Tergat's book. He's the Kenyan who holds the world's best marathon time of 2:04:55. Since he was at the race, he autographed a copy for me. The post-race goodie bag was also nice.

Running to Leadership

Several of us decided to wait for the final Texan to finish the race. Since the airlines had lost her luggage, she needed all the support she could get during the trip.

Today, we each joined the Seven Continents Club by completing a marathon on all seven continents. I've decided that I'd like to return to this marathon again. The experience was great.

Take care.

Post-Marathon Events

After the Kenyan marathon, I spent a week in Paris consolidating and writing two books about my global running and business experiences.

I returned to work from my scheduled vacation on July 2—my birthday. I was immediately laid off. What a birthday present!!! It's said, "When one door closes, bigger and better doors open." On the bright side, since I had been on vacation for two weeks, I didn't feel like my not-going-to-work habit was disrupted!!!

My girlfriend's daughter was getting married a few days later on 07/07/07. Since I had some "spare" time, I was immediately drafted in being their chauffer, table cloth ironer, wedding program designer and printer, and freelance photographer. It was fun and a great distraction. I jokingly said I could add these tasks to my resume and work for a wedding coordinator.

On the evening of the wedding, there was a Seven Continents celebration party. My girlfriend and I went from the wedding reception to the party and back to the post-wedding party. We must have driven over a hundred miles that afternoon and evening.

On July 17, a door opened. Thom Gilligan of Marathon Tours and Travel distributed the following press release.

FOR IMMEDIATE RELEASE

First Black Runner Finishes Seven Marathons on Seven Continents
Global Trail Blazer Heads Up National Black Marathoners' Association

BOSTON (July 17, 2007) – Tony Reed, the executive director and co-founder of the National Black Marathoners' Association (NBMA), has become the first Black runner to finish a marathon on all seven continents, announced Marathon Tours and Travel, a travel agency for marathon runners and organizer of the Seven Continents Club.

The Dallas-area runner has completed 26.2-mile jaunts in locales as far as flung the Great Wall of China, as icy as Antarctica and as precarious as an African game park. A finisher of over 87 marathons,

Running to Leadership

Reed wrapped up his seven-on-seven goal at the Safaricom Lewa Marathon in Kenya on June 23, 2007.

"Tony's spirit of adventure and love of the sport of running will no doubt motivate and inspire others in his community to pursue a healthy and active lifestyle," said Thom Gilligan, founder of Marathon Tours and Travel and its Seven Continents Club, a travel club for runners that offers special recognition for members who have completed seven marathons or seven half marathons on all seven continents.

Reed's international finishes include: the Cowtown Marathon (Ft. Worth, TX); Tailwinds Marathon (Copenhagen, Denmark); Gold Coast Marathon (Australia); Great Wall of China Marathon; Antarctic Marathon; Fin Del Mundo Marathon (Ushuaia, Argentina) and the Safaricom Lewa Marathon in Kenya.

Reed, who grew up in a St. Louis housing project, co-founded the National Black Marathoners' Association in 2004. The non-profit organization's mission is to encourage Black Americans to pursue a healthy lifestyle through running and to raise awareness of the health risks that are more prevalent among Blacks. The 500-member organization also awards college scholarships to high school distance runners.

"I was diagnosed with increased glucose levels but have been able to avoid full-blown diabetes by maintaining a healthy diet and by exercising," said Reed, who has a family history of the disease.

Running to Leadership

"I also want to set an example and inspire other Blacks to set and reach goals," said Reed, a speaker, an information technology consultant, and CPA who holds two masters and two bachelors degrees. The NBMA estimates that African Americans only make up one to two percent of all US marathoners.

Reflecting on his African continental finale, Reed said "The Safaricom Marathon was the first race I have ever been in where I did not feel like a minority."

For more information on Marathon Tours and Travel and the Seven Continents Club, please visit www.marathontours.com or call (617) 242-7845. For more information on the NBMA, visit www.BlackMarathoners.org.

A few days later, another door opened. Runner's World asked me to write an article about my experience in their website's First Person Blog section.

Running Along

102 Marathons Completed As Of 2011

Fastest Marathon Time
Age: 29
Date: December 2, 1984
Race: Dallas White Rock Marathon
Time: 3:36:45

Slowest Marathon Time
Age: 50
Date: May 20, 2006
Race: Great Wall of China Marathon
Time: 7:28:45
Note: I stopped and took over 100 photos during the
race

MARATHON (STATE)	YEARS	YRS
Ft Worth's Cowtown (TX)	1982, 83, 85–91, 93–96, 99, 2000, 03, 04, 08,09	19
Denton's NTSU (TX)	1982, 83	2
Wills Point's Day Break (TX)	1983	1
Dallas White Rock (TX)	1983–90, 92, 93, 95, 96, 98–00, 2003, 05–07, 08	20
San Antonio (TX)	1998, 99, 2003	3
Dallas Trails (TX)	1993, 99–01, 2003, 04	6
Houston (TX)	2000, 01, 03	3
Austin (TX)	2000, 01	2
Walk of Fame (TX)	2000	1

Running to Leadership

Chicago LaSalle (IL)	2000	1
New Orleans Mardi Gras (LA)	2001	1
Nashville's Country Music (TN)	2001	1
Pacific Shoreline (CA)	2004	1
Spirit of Saint Louis (MO)	2004, 06, 08	3
Race of Champions (MA)	2004	1
Tailwind Marathon (Denmark)	2004	1
Tupelo Marathon (MS)	2004	1
Oklahoma Marathon (Tulsa)	2004	1
Orange County Marathon (CA)	2004	1
Las Vegas Marathon (NV)	2005	1
Mercedes/Birmingham (AL)	2005	1
Little Rock (AR)	2005	1
Eisenhower (KS)	2005	1
Flying Pig (Cincinnati, OH)	2005	1
Keybank Vermont (VT)	2005	1
Gold Coast Airport (Australia)	2005	1
Iowa Trails 50K	2005	1
Lewis & Clark (MO)	2005	1
Hartford United Tech (CT)	2005	1
Myrtle Beach (SC)	2006	1
National (DC)	2006	1
New Jersey	2006	1
Great Wall of China	2006	1
New Mexico	2006	1
New Hampshire	2006	1
Tri-Cities (WA)	2006	1
Last Marathon (Antarctica)	2007	1
Fin Del Mundo (Argentina)	2007	1
ING Georgia (ATL)	2007	1
Salt Lake City (UT)	2007	1
Rite-Aid Cleveland	2007	1
Safaricom Lewa (Kenya)	2007	1
Heart of America (MO)	2007	1
Wineglass (NY)	2007	1
Philadelphia (PA)	2007	1

Lost Dutchman (AZ)	2008	1
Lincoln (NE)	2008	1
Denver (CO)	2008	1
Ultracentric Run (TX)	2008	1
Texas (TX)	2009	1
Deadwood-Michelson Trail (SD)	2010	1
Amica (RI)	2010	1

TOTAL MARATHONS   **102**

Selected Articles About Anthony Reed

- Winter, 2010/11 – Staring Down Danger, *Webster World.*
- December 2010/January 2011 – Marathons for a Good Cause, *Ebony.*
- August, 2010 - PMI New Jersey Chapter - Symposium and Seminar Offer, *PMI Today.*
- June 26, 2009 - Runner's Resume is Global, *Oak Cliff People.*
- May, 2009 - Body Talk - Ahead of the Pack, *Ebony.*
- February 24, 2009 - 100th Marathon Comes With A Cause, the *Dallas Morning News.*
- February 2, 2009 - Running Races For His Race, the *Ft. Worth Star-Telegram.*
- February, 2009 - Anthony Reed, *Black Sports - The Magazine.*
- Spring, 2008 - Staying the Course: Black Marathoners Share Lessons from the Race, *Black MBA Magazine.*
- February 2008 – "Human Race: Equal Footing," *Runners World.*
- November, 2007 – "The Last Word," *The Journal of Accountancy.*

Running to Leadership

- August, 2007 – "First Black Runner Finishes Marathon on all Seven Continents," *Runner Triathlete News*.
- July 17, 2007 – "Tony Reed Becomes First Black Runner To Finish Seven Marathons On Seven Continents," *Runners World*.
- July 17, 2007 – "Tony Reed: How I Became the First Black Runner to Complete Marathons on All Seven Continents," *Runners World*.
- May 18, 2007 – "Cleveland Marathon: A Foot Soldier for Blacks' Good Health," *The Plain Dealer* (Cleveland, OH).
- May/June, 2007 – "The Antarctica Marathon – The Marathon Texans Loved to Hate," *Inside Texas Running*.
- March 16, 2007 – "Some Cold Feet, But No Weak Knees – Antarctica Marathon," *The Dallas Morning News*.
- First Quarter, 2007 – "A Success Story – The Running Man," *Texins Magazine*.
- Fall, 2006 – "Great Wall Delivers a Great Adventure," *Travel News For Runners*.
- Sep/Oct, 2005 - NBMA to Gather at Lewis & Clark Marathon," *Missouri Runner and Triathlete*.
- February 28, 2005 – "A Brief Chat with Tony Reed," Runners World.
- January 30, 2005 – "Runners Keep Sport in Step with Times," The Ft. Worth (TX) *Star-Telegram*.
- April 25 and 26, 2005 – "Promoting Healthier Lives & Related Editorial," *The Cincinnati Enquirer*.
- March 5, 2004 – "Diabetes Hasn't Caught Up To Local Marathoner," *The Dallas Morning News*.
- March 3, 2004 – "50 Was Nifty for Dallas Marathoner," *The Ft. Worth Star-Telegram*.
- March, 2004 - featured as "*CPA and Former Wyman Camper and Counselor*" in Cornerstone for Kids campaign in support of Wyman and Camp Coca-Cola.
- Summer, 2003 - "Management Consultant Spends Free Time Running Marathons" *Webster (University) World*.

Running to Leadership

- March 28, 2003 – "Marathoner Reaches Goal Before 50," *The Dallas Morning News* Sports Section.
- July 28, 2002 – "IT Success Story," *Dallas Morning News*.
- November 19, 1999 – "TemporaryCIO.com review," *Dallas Business News* High-Tech Section.
- December, 1985 – "A Tale of Two Athletes," *News at 11K*.